Women and asian martial traditions

An Anthology of
Articles from the
Journal of Asian Martial Arts
Compiled by Michael A. DeMarco, M.A.

Disclaimer
Please note that the authors and publisher of this book are not responsible in any manner whatsoever for any injury that may result from practicing the techniques and/or following the instructions given within. Since the physical activities described herein may be too strenuous in nature for some readers to engage in safely, it is essential that a physician be consulted prior to training.

All Rights Reserved
No part of this publication, including illustrations, may be reproduced or utilized in any form or by any means, electronic or mechanical, including photocopying, recording, or by any information storage and retrieval system (beyond that copying permitted by sections 107 and 108 of the US Copyright Law and except by reviewers for the public press), without written permission from Via Media Publishing Company.

Warning: Any unauthorized act in relation to a copyright work may result in both a civil claim for damages and criminal prosecution.

Copyright © 2016 by
Via Media Publishing Company
941 Calle Mejia #822
Santa Fe, NM 87501 USA
E-mail: md@goviamedia.com

All articles in this anthology were originally published in the *Journal of Asian Martial Arts*.
Listed according to the table of contents for this anthology:

Amdur, E. (1996)	Vol. 5 No. 2	p. 10-35
Yao, H. (2001)	Vol. 10 No. 1	p. 18-35
Mukhopadhyay, B. (2002)	Vol. 11 No. 2	p. 50-63
Finch, D. (2003)	Vol. 12 No. 1	p. 40-47
Soderholm, M. (2004)	Vol. 13 No. 1	p. 56-63
Vogel, R. (2005)	Vol. 14 No. 3	p. 30-37
Finch, D. (2006)	Vol. 15 No. 2	p. 60-69
Henning, S. (2007)	Vol. 16 No. 3	p. 26-29
Klens-Bigman, D., (2010)	Vol. 19 No. 3	p. 65-77
Schneider, S. (2010)	Vol. 19 No. 3	p. 46-63
Sheetz-Runkle, B. (2011)	Vol. 20 No. 4	p. 80-97
Pauka, K. (2003),	Vol. 12 No. 1	p. 48-65

Book and cover design by Via Media Publishing Company
Edited by Michael A. DeMarco, M.A.

Cover illustration
Courtesy of Masterfile.com
© Masterfile

ISBN: 978-1893765283

w w w . v i a m e d i a p u b l i s h i n g . c o m

contents

iv **Preface**
by Michael DeMarco, M.A.

CHAPTERS

1   The Role of Arms-Bearing Women in Japanese History
    by Ellis Amdur, M.A.

37 Martial-Acrobatic Arts in Peking Opera
    With a Brief Analysis of Fighting Movement
    by Haishing Yao, Ph.D.

57 War and Worship: Evolution of Martial Music and Dance in India
    by Bandana Mukhopadhyay, Ph.D.

73 Ulla Werbrouck: Olympic and European Judo Champion Retires
    by David Finch

79 The Art of Conversation: Random Flow Training
    in Visayan Corto Kadena Eskrima
    by Majia Soderholm, B.Sc.

88 The Ki to a Lasting Marriage: The Application of
    Internal Martial Arts Principles in the Marital Dojo
    by Richard Vogel, Ph.D.

97 North Korean Kye Sun Hui: An Extraordinary Olympic Judo Player
    by David Finch

102 The Maiden of Yue: Fount of Chinese Martial Arts Theory
    by Stanley E. Henning, M.A.

107 Fighting Women of Kabuki Theater
    and the Legacy of Women's Japanese Martial Arts
    by Deborah Klens-Bigman, Ph.D.

120 Learning India's Martial Art of Kalarippayattu:
    Unsettled Ecologies of Gender, Class, Culture, and Ethnicity
    by Sara K. Schneider, Ph.D.

138 Why Women Need Sunzi's Book *The Art of War*
    by Becky Sheetz-Runkle, B.A.

154 Silat-Based Randai Theatre of West Sumatra Makes Its U.S. Debut
    by Kirsten Pauka, Ph.D.

168 **Index**

preface

This anthology is filled with content specifically selected for readers who have a strong interest in women's participation in the Asian martial traditions. In addition to combative theory and practice, topics include aspects of theatrical performance, music, dance, gender studies, and insights for embodying philosophical elements into daily life. The twelve chapters that were written by noted authorities will certainly educate and inspire. These focus on the martial traditions of Japan, China, India, Korea, Indonesia, and the Philippines.

To identify with one's predecessors is a strong desire for most people. For many women, particularly those interested in Japanese martial practice, there is the image of the woman warrior bearing a naginata in the protection of her home, and even on the field of battle. In the first chapter, Ellis Amdur provides an excellent historical overview and a presentation of modern female headmasters.

Fighting movement is perhaps the most fascinating element of Peking Opera performance. Dr. Haishing Yao explores the significance of these arts and the different layers of meaning they represent. The intense training for performing the martial-acrobatic arts are discussed in detail and selected movements demonstrated.

Dr. Mukhopadhyay states that Indian martial arts survive primarily among the indigenous tribal communities where martial dance and music are both acts of ritual to appease nature and she shows how this manifests as entertainment for the community. In another chapter Dr. Schneider discusses her field experience studying kalarippayattu. She examines the complexities of communication in an intercultural teacher-student relationship, and how gender, culture, and class impacted learning in this embodied art form.

David Finch, famed photographer and authority on judo topics, details the Olympic competitions of champions Ulla Webrouck and Kye Sun Hui. His two chapters highlight the major accomplishments of their international careers and describes some of their judo skills in obtaining their Olympic titles.

Moving into Filipino traditions, Majia Soderholm presents the art of Visayan Corto Kadena Eskrima and some of its concepts and training methods with regard to free-sparring with swords. It is a Filipino martial system encompassing empty-hand and non-bladed and bladed weapons.

As a psychologist who has specialized in marital therapy for twenty years, Dr. Vogel found that the application of the practice and the metaphysical underpinnings of internal martial arts systems can restore and perpetuate goodwill between embattled spouses. The main concepts for his chapter were derived from taijiquan, aikido, and the *Book of Changes* (*Yijing*).

The Maiden of Yue story is presented by Stanley Henning. It is a tale that explains the essence of Chinese martial arts theory. It is the earliest such description in Chinese history and has been paraphrased by other martial artists over the centuries. The story describes both internal and external characteristics that combine mental and physical attributes.

The fighting woman character has always been a staple of Japan's kabuki theater. Audiences accepted these characters as part of the depiction of Edo period (1603–1868) life. The chapter by Dr. Klens-Bigman explores several of these characters and suggests that they help form the legacy of women's practice of martial arts today.

The Art of War has much to teach women martial artists about how to train to be effective in a life-or-death encounter. Preparation for this chapter was derived from author Becky Sheetz-Runkle's research, plus the her years of training against much larger and stronger opponents, and years of teaching martial arts, particularly aikijujutsu.

The closing chapter by Dr. Kirsten Pauka deals with a colorful martially-inspired art. Randai theater is fundamentally based on silat, the indigenous martial art found throughout Malaysia and Indonesia. Besides martial arts, Randai features dance, acting, singing, and instrumental music. This chapter reports on an extended artist-in-residence program in the Asian Theatre Program at the University of Hawai'i.

The above summary of chapters hint at the richness of content being shared in this anthology. All of the historical and cultural details add much to the scholarly perspectives on these Asian arts. At the same time they add to the appreciation of how and why martial elements are infused in artistic performances, such as theater, music, and dance. Throughout can be seen the unifying thread of the womans' role which will increase our appreciation of the feminine presence in Asian martial traditions.

Michael A. DeMarco, Publisher
Santa Fe, New Mexico
July 2016

Notes

· 1 ·

The Role of the Arms-Bearing Women in Japanese History

by Ellis Amdur, M.A.

Tomoe Gozen from Kuniyoshi's "One Hundred Heroes Story." As is usually the case, Tomoe Gozen is drawn bearing a naginata although there is no record of her ever using this weapon. Nonetheless, this portrait clearly gives evidence of the admiration with which the Japanese regarded this legendary woman. *Courtesy of the Tokyo Central Library.*

Introduction

The entry of Asian martial arts into the Western world happens to have coincided, through no particular design, with the transformation of women's role in society. Women of the early 21st century have risen into prominence in business, science, and as players on the political stage. The victimization of women in domestic violence and sexual and physical assault is still rampant, but it is increasingly countered through legislation and political activism and, on a personal level, through women's pursuit of fighting skills to defend themselves. Ever greater numbers of women are involved in martial arts, self-defense and firearms training.

For most people, identifying with one's predecessors is a strong desire. One often models oneself on an ideal that is personified in heroic myths or tales. Many women interested in Japanese martial practice find images and stories of women warriors bearing a naginata in the protection of her home and even on the field of battle. Yet, although it is a glorious image, it is difficult to separate fact from fancy because of the almost complete absence of historical records that document the role of arms-bearing women.

Early History

The battle tales of Japan, chronicles of wars in the Heian, Kamakura, and Muromachi periods, focus almost completely on the deeds of the nobility and the warrior class. These tales, passed down by blind bards much as in Homer's *Iliad*, present warriors as archetypes: the Tragic-Heroic-Loser, the Warrior-Courtier, the Loyal-Unto-Death Servitor, the Traitor, the Coward, etc. Women warriors are almost never described or even mentioned.

Women's roles in such tales are slight: the Tragic Heroine who kills herself at the death of her husband; the Loyal Wife who is taken captive; the Stalwart Mother who grooms her son to take vengeance for his father's death; the Vengeful Temptress; the Merciful Woman whose 'weak' and 'feminine' qualities may encourage, for example, a warrior chieftain to indulge in unmanly sympathy and dissuade him from slaughtering his enemy's children, who later grow up to kill him; and the Seductress who preoccupies the warrior leader and diverts him from his task with her feminine wiles. Finally, almost casually mentioned, are women *en masse*: either slaughtered or 'given' to the warriors as 'spoils-of-war.' That they were surely raped and often murdered was apparently considered too trivial a fact to even mention in later warrior tales, once the conventions of the genre had been codified, just as the wholesale burning and pillaging of peasants' farms was considered such a matter of course that it ceased to be mentioned, as if such repeated references would only disturb the flow of narrative. Unless one is willing to imagine a conspiracy of silence in which women's role on the battlefield was suppressed in both historical records and battle-tales, it is a fair assumption that *onna-musha* (women warriors) were very unusual. This is borne out, I believe, by the prominence given to the few women about whom accounts are written. The most famous women warriors are Tomoe Gozen and Hangaku Gozen (sometimes called Itagaki). Given the stereotype of the naginata as a 'woman's weapon,' it is interesting to note that the naginata was not associated with either of them.

In the *Heike Monogatari*, Tomoe Gozen appears as a general in the troops of Kiso Yoshinaka, Yoritomo's first attack force. She was described as follows:

Tomoe was especially beautiful, with white skin, long hair, and charming features. She was also a remarkably strong archer, and as a swords-woman she was a warrior worth a thousand, ready to confront a demon or a god, mounted or on foot. She handled unbroken horses with superb skill; she rode unscathed down perilous descents. Whenever a battle was imminent, Yoshinaka sent her out as his first captain, equipped with strong armor, an oversized sword, and a mighty bow; and she performed more deeds of valor than any of his other warriors.[1]

Her last act, on the verge of Yoshinaka's defeat, is the subject of many plays and poems. To buy time for her husband to commit *seppuku* (ritual suicide), she rode into the enemy forces and, flinging herself on their strongest warrior, unhorsed, pinned, and decapitated him.

In the interim, however, Yoshinaka was killed by an arrow. Conflicting legends attest that she was killed, that she survived to become a Buddhist nun, or that she was taken captive by Wada Yoshimori and with him, had a son, Asahina, considered to be the strongest warrior of the later Kamakura era.

However, Tomoe has not ever been proven to be an historical figure—and this was not for lack of trying. She has exerted a fascination upon the Japanese for hundreds of years in the startling image of a beauteous woman who was also a breaker of wild horses and the equal of any man. Tomoe is claimed by more than a few naginata traditions to be either their founder or one of their primordial teachers. There is, however, no historical justification for such claims. She lived centuries before their martial traditions were even dreamed of, and is not even described as ever wielding a naginata.

The second famous woman warrior is Hangaku Gozen, daughter of the Jo, a warrior family of Echigo province. She was known for her strength and accuracy with the bow and arrow. In 1201, after the feudal government attempted to subjugate one of her nephews, the warriors of Echigo and Shinano revolted. Besieged in Torizakayama, she held off the enemy from the roof of a storehouse. After being wounded in both legs by spears and arrows, she was taken prisoner. Drawn by her beauty and dignity, Asari Yoshito of the Kai Genji courted her and they married. According to some account, they lived the rest of their lives in peace. Others assert that she was killed while assisting in the defense of Torizakayama Castle.

Thus, at least in the earlier periods such as the Heian and Kamakura, women who became prominent or even present on the field of battle were the exception rather than the rule. This does not indicate, however, that most women were powerless. There is a common image of Japanese femininity based on the accounts we have of women of the Imperial Court, swaddled in layers of kimono and rigid custom, preoccupied with poetry and moon viewing. But such a picture obscures just who the bushi women were during the ascendancy of their class. They were originally pioneers, helping to settle new lands and, if need be, fighting, like women of the old western territories in American history. Some bushi clans may even have been led by women. This can be inferred from the legal right given to women to function as *jito* (stewards), who supervised land held in absentia by nobles or temples.

The Warring States Period

From the tenth century on, Japan can never be said to have been at peace, but in 1467, the whole country was engulfed what became known as the *Sengoku Jidai* (Warring States Period, circa 1467 through 1573). It was a time in which all social classes were caught up into war. Feudal domains were sometimes stripped of almost all healthy men, who had hired themselves out as mercenaries, taken to brigandage, were drafted into armies, or slaughtered in battle. As a result of this rampant warfare, women were often the last defense of towns and castles.

In this period there are accounts of the wives of warlords, dressed in flamboyant armor, leading bands of women armed with naginata. Accord-

A Night Attack on the Horikawa by Yoshitora. Women often became part of the last line of defense when a castle or manor was under attack. *Courtesy of the Tokyo Central Library.*

ing to long-standing oral tradition, bushi women were trained with the naginata because of its versatility against all manner of enemies and weapons. It was generally the responsibility of women to protect their homes rather than go off to battle, so it was important that they become skilled in a few weapons that offered the best range of techniques to defend against marauders who often attacked on horseback. Therefore, it makes sense that women were sometimes adept with the bow due to its effectiveness at long-range and often with the naginata as it was an effective weapon against horse riders at closer range. Most women are weakest at close quarters where men can bring their greater weight and strength to bear. A strong, lithe woman armed with a naginata could keep all but the best warriors at a distance, where the advantages of strength, weight, or sword counted for less.

In an account in the *Bichi Hyoranki*, for example, the wife of Mimura Kotoku, appalled by the mass suicide of the surviving women and children in her husband's besieged castle, armed herself and led eighty-three soldiers against the enemy, 'whirling her naginata like a waterwheel.' She challenged a mounted general, Ura Hyobu, but he refused, claiming that women were unfit as opponents to true warriors. He edged backwards in cowardice, saying under his breath, "She is a demon!" She refused to back down, but while his soldiers attacked her, he escaped. She cut through her attackers and won her way back to the castle.

It was probably at this time that the image of women fighters with naginata arose. However, as Yazawa Isao, a sixteenth-generation headmistress of Toda-ha Buko-ryu wrote,[2] the main weapon of most women in these horrible times was not the naginata, but the *kaiken*, which bushi women carried at all times. Yazawa stated that a woman was not usually expected to fight with her dagger. Instead, she was required to kill herself in a manner as wrapped in custom as the male warrior's seppuku. In seppuku, a man was required to show his stoicism in the face of unimaginable pain by disemboweling himself. Women, however, were expected to use their dagger to cut their carotid artery, thereby having a method in which death would occur relatively quickly. The nature of the wound was not likely to cause an ugly distortion of the features or disarrangement of the limbs that would offend the woman's dignity after death.

Women did not train in using the kaiken with sophisticated combat techniques either. If a woman were forced to fight, she was to grab the hilt with both hands, plant the butt firmly against her stomach, and run forward to stab the enemy with all her weight behind the blade. She was to become, for a moment, a living spear. Rather than boldly drawing her dagger and challenging her enemy, she had to find some way to catch him unawares. Were she successful, she would most likely be unstoppable. More often than not, however, a woman could not expect to face a single foe nor, even then, to have the advantage of surprise. If she were captured alive, even after killing several enemies, she would be raped, displayed as a captive, or otherwise dishonored. In the rigid beliefs of this period, women would thereby allow shame to attach to their name. The only escape from what was believed to be disgrace was death at one's own hands.

The Edo Period: An Enforced Peace

In the mid-seventeen century, when Japan finally arrived at an enforced peace under the rule of the Tokugawa shogunate, the need for skill at arms decreased. The turbulent energies of the warrior class were restrained by an intricate code of conduct based upon laws governing behavior appropriate to each level of society. The rough codes of earlier warriors were roughly codified into doctrines governing all behavior, eventually referred to as *bushido* (the 'way of the warrior'). Self-sacrifice, honor, and loyalty became fixed ideals, focusing the energies of the warrior class on a new role as governing bureaucrats and police agents. The role of the bushi was mythologized, and certain images held up as ideals for all to emulate. That these doctrines were primarily a Confucian political ideology rather than a way for active warriors to survive is shown by the fact that the original reference to these codes was *shido* (in Chinese, the way of the 'gentleman'), a direct reference to Confucian concepts.

Everyone was required to fill an immutable role in society, fixed at birth and held until death. The rules and social conventions governing conduct between men and women, formerly somewhat more egalitarian, became more rigid than in any other period of Japanese history. A woman's relationship towards her husband was said to mirror that of a samurai towards his lord. The bushi woman was expected to center her life around her home, serving her family in the person of her husband first, his sons second, and her mother-in-law third. Work was almost completely gender divided, and the lives of men and women became increasingly separate from one another. There was usually a room in each house reserved for men which women were forbidden to enter, even to clean or serve food. Husbands and wives did not even customarily sleep together. The husband would visit his wife to initiate any sexual activity and afterwards would retire to his own room.

The legends of women warriors defending their homes and their families became means to define a woman's role in society. They trained with the naginata less to prepare for combat than to instill them with the idealized virtues necessary to be a samurai wife. A women's work was unremitting service to the males of the household and tireless effort to teach proper behavior to her children, who were legally considered to be her husband's alone. However, unlike the upper-class women of Victorian England, who were expected to be subservient and frail, the bushi women were expected to be subservient and strong. Their duty was to endure.

When a bushi woman married, one of the possessions that she took to her husband's home was a naginata. Like the *daisho* (long and short swords) that her husband bore, the naginata was considered an emblem of her role in society. Practice with the naginata was a means of merging with a spirit of self-sacrifice, of connecting with the hallowed ideals of the warrior class. As men were expected to sacrifice themselves for the state and the maintenance of society, women were expected to sacrifice themselves to a rigid, limited life in the home.[3] No longer carried on the battlefield or even considered a weapon of war,[4] the use of the naginata was confined to practice with wooden replicas in the many martial traditions.

In the mostly peaceful years of the Edo period, martial systems, once comprehensive systems encompassing a variety of weapons, fissioned, each faction specializing in one or another weapon. Many schools focusing on the use of the naginata were created and, as the Edo period progressed, these schools began to be increasingly associated with women.

In more rural areas, however, women maintained an active role in maintaining order. The mother of one of my instructors told how when she was a small girl in a village in Kyushu, men were often gone from the village in certain seasons to join up on labor crews. When there was a disturbance at night or a suspicious character entered the village, the women would grab their naginata, which hung ready on one of the walls of their houses, and go running outside to gather and search the town for any danger. Her grandmother was the leader of this 'emergency response squad,' a naturally autonomous group within the village. Protecting the neighborhood was simply assumed to be one of their responsibilities.

A Last Battle: Nakano Takeko

The last time that the naginata is known to have figured in actual battle was the *Boshin Senso*, the civil war that led to the overthrow of the Tokugawa shogunate, and the restoration of power, ostensibly to the Emperor.

Both sides used modern weaponry, including cannons, Gatling guns, and rifles. The Imperial forces, however, had far more. Contrary to many romantic accounts, both sides had foreign military advisors as well. Nonetheless, traditional weaponry was also used in hand-to-hand battle—or more often, those wielding traditional weaponry attempted to engage in hand-to-hand battle, only to be decimated by firearms.

One of the final battles of this war was the campaign against the Aizu feudal domain. Aizu had always been a fiercely traditional place, and it was far more scrupulous in training its young warriors, including women, throughout the Edo period. Among the latter was Nakano Takeko.

Nakano was raised in Edo, the daughter of an Aizu councilor, Nakano Heinai. She was trained in both literary and martial arts by Akaoka Daisuke.[5] One source asserts that she was trained in a faction of Itto-ryu.[6] Although Itto-ryu is generally considered to be a kenjutsu school, many branches also trained in other weapons, including the naginata. Her sister, Yuko and mother, Koko were also skilled with the naginata. Nakano was also known as an exemplar of discipline, making one thousand sword-cuts every day.[7]

According to another source, Nakano was trained specifically in naginata by Kurokochi Dengoro, the leading martial arts teacher of the Aizu.[8] Kurokochi, the maternal grandfather of Takeda Sokaku, of Daito-ryu fame, was, among a number of attainments, an expert at Anazawa-ryu. However, because she only returned to Aizu in 1868, she would only have possibly had brief tutelage from Kurokochi.

Upon her return to Aizu, she formed a women's battalion, numbering twenty, all of whom trained with the naginata. They first served as bodyguards for Matsudaira Teruhime, the adoptive sister of Matsudaira Katamori, the leader of the Aizu domain.

As the Aizu were being overrun, Nakano mustered her battalion, and entered the fighting at Yanagibayashi. They charged a group of enemy riflemen, trying to break through their lines. Nakano was shot in the chest. Borne away from the front lines, she demanded that her sister behead her, lest she be captured alive and thereby dishonored. She was only twenty-two years old.

Some of the Joshitai survived. They were regarded as honorable heroes rather than traitors. Even the Imperial government later awarded medals to some of these women, most notably the remarkable Yamamoto Yaeko. A discussion of Yamamoto's life deserves a book in itself, but confining ourselves to the period of the Boshin Senso, she, too, was a woman of valor, one very different from Nakano. The daughter of one of the gunnery instructors of the Aizu domain, she served as a sharpshooter, armed with a Spencer repeating rifle rather than a naginata. She fought to win and survive, rather than lose her life in glorious sacrifice.[9]

Tendo-ryu: One Foot on the Battlefield, One in the Modern World

Tendo-ryu naginatajutsu exemplifies many of the most significant changes that occurred in martial training from the late sixteenth century to the present. These include:

- the transition from a warrior's art incorporating many weapons to a martial tradition with a decided emphasis on a single one;
- the increasing perception of the naginata as a weapon associated with women;
- the transition of martial arts from combative training to a training of will and spirit;
- the use of martial arts training in mass education;
- the development of sportive forms of martial training.

The founder of Tendo-ryu is said to be Saito Denkibo Katsuhide. His original school, Ten-ryu was developed sometime in the 1560s, a time of chaos and warfare. Some traditions state that he studied with Tsukahara Bokuden, the founder of Kashima Shinto-ryu. Legends of Ten-ryu assert that Saito went into retreat at a shrine in Kamakura. One night, in an incident curiously reminiscent of the Biblical tale of Jacob wrestling with the angel, he got into a fight with a mountain ascetic. After a battle lasting until dawn, Saito asked his opponent his school's name. Saying nothing, the man walked away towards the sun. In a moment of inspiration, Saito realized the name of the school he would soon develop to be Ten-ryu, 'Heaven's Tradition.'

This story is illustrative of the fact that an 'enlightenment' experience does not necessarily endow an individual with any moral virtues. Saito remained a flamboyant, pugnacious man. In some accounts, he is described wearing a kimono in imitation of feathers as if he were a tengu. After many duels, he killed his last opponent at the age thirty-eight. He was later ambushed by the dead man's followers, who fired arrows from several directions. He was able to knock down many of the arrows with a *kamayari* (long-hafted sickle) but finally was killed, "as full of arrows as a hedgehog has quills" as one modern authority put it. Saito's arrow-blocking method supposedly became the basis of some of the central techniques of Tendo-ryu naginatajutsu.

Ten-ryu had a rather violent history during the Edo period and quite a few of its members were involved in well-known duels with people from other schools.

Ten-ryu included the study of a number of weapons—their kenjutsu, in particular, became renowned. The oldest records of the school include instructions for the study of sword and numerous other weapons, as well as battlefield tactics, fighting on horseback, hand-to-hand combat, and esoteric philosophical teachings. Over time, the ryu split into a number of lines that specialized in sword, spear, or other weapons. Mitamura Kengyo, headmaster of one line in the late 1800s, singled out the naginata particularly for the training of women and girls. Mitamura's line, at some point, began to refer to their tradition as Tendo-ryu, 'The Tradition of the Way of Heaven.'

Mitamura helped organize the *Seitokusha*, a school of Shinto and martial arts practice in an effort to combat the steady influx of Western influence. In 1895, his group merged with the *Dai Nippon Butokukai*, a national regulating body of martial arts. After displaying his methods for group teaching in 1899, he was contracted by the large Doshisha women's school in Kyoto to teach on a regular basis. Women took prominence as teachers (most notably, Mitamura's brilliant wife, Mitamura Chiyo), and the practice weapon was made lighter.[10]

There are 120 two-person kata surviving, featuring the naginata, sword, kusarigama, jo (mid-length staff), two swords, and short sword. The person in the teaching position, called *uketachi* (receiving sword), is always armed with a sword. The instructor's function is to serve as 'cooperative opposition,' thereby enabling the students to hone their skills.

Most forms feature the naginata as *shitachi* (user's sword), which is the learner's role. It is unclear when these forms were developed, although it is quite unusual for older martial systems to contain so many kata emphasizing a single weapon such as the naginata. It is thus a fair surmise that more forms were probably added over time as practitioners attempted to add either their personal stamp or more sophistication to the curriculum of the school.

Ichi Monji no Midare. This kata is one of the most important in Tendo-ryu and serves as the basis for many other more complex forms. It is this form which is said to have been derived from the arrow-deflecting technique of Saito Denkibo. *Artwork courtesy of Shinji Marumori.*

Group training in the Shubukan Dojo in Osaka, 1982, under the direction of headmistress Mitamura Takeko. *Photos courtesy of E. Amdur.*

The techniques are first practiced singly and then, after a time, with a partner. Several decades ago, I observed the midsummer practice at the Shubukan Dojo near Osaka, where practitioners from all over Japan gather to train together. One of my enduring memories of this school was the sight of perhaps one hundred women, under the direction of 16th generation headmistress Mitamura Takeko, granddaughter of Mitamura Kengyo and Mitamura Chiyo, cutting and thrusting through their basic techniques in sweeping arcs of perfect unity.

The basic forms are a series of crisp, spiraling movements of the naginata against the sword. These naginata forms often utilize cuts to the wrist or underarm. Ichi Monji no midare, the technique Saito Denkibo is said to have used to cut down arrows 400 years ago, forms the basis for many kata.

Although the roots of Tendo-ryu were developed during a time of war, many of the techniques of the original Ten-ryu have surely been abandoned or lost. In spite of this, the people who practice Tendo-ryu today have been able to maintain a large part of the spirit and frame of reference of those times. The kata are practiced to instill a sense of fighting awareness. Mitamura Takeko called it the 'cut and thrust spirit.' She believes that practicing in this way can help one to reach deep inside oneself. "I don't just practice the naginata; it is a part of me." She stated that even though a student practices killing, "the gentleness and softness inherent in a woman is not lost. In fact, the training is aimed at focusing those traits into a strength which can be used for fostering and protecting as well as taking life."

The instructor usually initiates the kata, maintaining a spacing perhaps one half step outside that which would be appropriate to strike the practitioner. Tendo-ryu found this necessary because otherwise the naginata wielder's movements might become cramped and abbreviated as she tried to safely accommodate her cuts so as not to strike the instructor standing within range. Thus, Tendo-ryu's forms are geared to the development of the naginata's technique, allowing the practitioner to cut with full power and extension.

The attacker, with the sword, while trying to draw and lead the practitioner, is by no means passive. Instructors constantly remind their students that both sides must attack, not receive. There are two main *kiai*, (use of the voice and breath to create or foster certain physical organization or reactions within oneself or one's opponents), one for calling or pulling your opponent toward you (TOH!) and the deciding kiai. This final kiai is executed in two ways: a short forceful "EEIIH!" to accompany and strengthen cuts and a piercing 'spiraling' manner "Eeeihhh!" to enhance thrusts. Smoothness of breath and the maintenance of postural integrity while breathing deeply are emphasized.

Perfect combat spacing between headmistress Mitamura Takeko (sword) and Sawada Hanae (naginata). *Photo courtesy of the Nippon Budokan.*

Some of the kata, featuring both naginata and short sword, are realistic about the limitations of the long weapon. Since the naginata is not very effective in close fighting, it is thrown aside as the swordfighter gets inside its arc. The short sword is quickly drawn and used to stab the swordfighter. This type of form harkens back to two sources: combative grappling, in which fighters would use small weapons on the belt, and the use of the dagger by women fighting an opponent who attempted to use his greater mass and skill at close combat to overwhelm her.

Some of the senior practitioners still train in the other weapons of the school. These include techniques with the chain-and-sickle, a five-foot staff that simulates the haft of a naginata with the blade broken off, and some very intriguing forms featuring two swords.

Tendo-ryu's main dojo is the Shubukan in Osaka, but there are powerful groups in many other areas of Japan. The members, almost all women, ranging from slender and young to stout and old, are not exceedingly formal. There is much laughter, affection, and love. But during the practice of the kata, there is a razor-sharp focus found in few dojos anywhere. Unlike some schools, which claim to have remained largely unchanged since their inception, it is likely that Tendo-ryu is far different than the original Ten-ryu practiced by the wild Saito Denkibo Katsuhide. Nonetheless, perhaps the best of his spirit still resides in the hands and hearts of the women of Tendo-ryu, a courage and integrity in movement anyone would do well to emulate.

The Development of Naginata in the Meiji Period: Jikishinkage-ryu Naginata-do

At roughly the same time that Mitamura Kengyo and other teachers were initiating a renaissance in Tendo-ryu, another remarkable school of naginata, the Jikishinkage-ryu naginata-do was born. This school claims its roots in Kashima Shinden Jikishinkage-ryu. Although this tradition traces a lineage back to the famous Shinto-ryu swordsman, Matsumoto Bizen no Kami, it was most likely developed by a monk Yamada Heizaemon Mitsunori (Ippusai), usually regarded as the seventh generation headmaster, out of elements of older Shinkage-ryu and Shinto-ryu sword schools. Ippusai's ryu, one of the most significant of the Edo and Meiji periods, has deep connections with esoteric and mystical teachings and was one of the first schools to engage in competitive practice with split bamboo swords.

Kashima Shinden Jikishinkage-ryu is famous for a cryptic set of kata, called Hojo, executed with massive wooden swords, which seem to be created for the development of power, coupled with very sophisticated kiaijutsu. The ryu also has a number of ritual movements, which, like the aforementioned kata, are utterly unique to the school. Kashima Shinden Jikishinkage-ryu is, in so many ways, a one-of-a-kind tradition, instantly recognizable to those familiar with Japanese martial arts. It is for that reason that a claim that Jikishinkage-ryu naginata-do has descended from this school is quite surprising because it has none of the ritual practices nor esoteric teachings, and perhaps more importantly, practitioners do not use their bodies or weaponry in any way similar to Kashima Shinden Jikishinkage-ryu.

What we do know is this: in the 1860s, Satake Yoshinori developed or revealed a hitherto-unseen school with his wife, Satake Shigeo. She had studied martial arts since she was six years old and was famous for her skill with the naginata. Yoshinori is usually claimed to have studied Kashima Shinden Jikishinkage-ryu, although there are no records to establish this.

There is also anecdotal evidence that both practiced *gekiken*, the precursor to modern kendo. One historian who has researched the school in some depth informed me that she believed the Ryugo-ryu, a school infamous for winning matches using *shinai* (split bamboo replica sword) anywhere from four to six feet long (approximately 120-183 cm), was, in fact, the true primary influence on the development of this school. In addition to its use of a very long shinai, the ryu was known for its attacks to the lower legs, a technique for which Jikishinkage-ryu naginata-do later became famous. The way that the naginata is wielded in Jikishinkage-ryu is congruent with this theory: the very light wooden practice weapon is held at the very end and cuts often look far more like sword/shinai cuts than those of a heavy glaive.

The fifteenth generation headmistress, Sonobe Hideo, was adopted into the Satake's family. As far as is known, it was Sonobe who consolidated the ryu in its present form, with its twenty-five naginata against sword kata. Sonobe was considered a master at naginata, one of perhaps the two or three best women naginata practitioners of the prewar era. One high-ranking iaido and kendo instructor of the era still remembers her appearing at exhibitions at the old *Butokuden*, the great training hall of the Dai Nippon Butokukai. He said top ranking kendo practitioners were scared of her. She was so tough she was "like a man. She could beat nearly any kendo person she went up against."

Sonobe took Jikishinkage-ryu into girls' schools. She taught at major schools in the Kyoto area and was one of the first teachers to popularize mass training. The system has continued to grow and has the most students of any of the traditional schools of naginata. Sonobe was followed by her son, Sonobe Shigehachi and his wife, Asano. Her leading student, however, was probably Shimada Teruko, a descendent of the Yamauchi, former daimyo of Tosa-han.

Shimada was described as being as fearsome as Sonobe, but also bearing an air of elegance and nobility. The seventeenth generation headmistress was Toya Akiko, who led the school when I visited in the 1980's. The present headmaster is Sonobe Masami, who married into and was adopted within the family line.

Training in Jikishinkage-ryu naginata-do and on the following page is headmistress Toya Akiko with the chain-and-sickle.

Headmistress Toya Akiko and senior instructor Higashi Tomoko in Jikishinkage-ryu Naginata-do. *Photos courtesy of E. Amdur.*

When I observed the school in the 1980's, the emphasis appears to be on correct performance rather than development of martial skills. The forms of Jikishinkage-ryu are done in straight lines in a highly defined rhythm. The kiai is traded back and forth, in almost a call-and-response, adding to a sense of dance-like structure. The forms project an aura of crisp elegance. When a mistake was made in the practices that I observed, the kata was discontinued and started over. Even senior teachers seemed unable to respond spontaneously to unexpected movements by their partners. Thus, it seems to me that perfection of the form rather than an ability to improvise freely is the aim of the school.

Their naginata is a very light, relatively short weapon, held in a rather narrow grip at one end of the haft and whirled around a central axis. The curve of the blade is not used to deflect attacks of the sword, and the cuts and thrusts are straight. The practice weapon is so light and slender that one could easily see it as a descendent of practices with a long shinai rather than an actual naginata.

Almost all the forms are oriented towards practice for the naginata, with the sword merely receiving attacks. There are also a few collateral forms featuring a highly stylized practice of the kusarigama against the sword, the practice weapon with a cord rather than a chain. The spacing between the partners is such that it is unlikely that the sword would be able to strike a damaging blow in most circumstances.

Despite its seemingly non-combative orientation, Jikishinkage-ryu first made its name in matches against kendo practitioners. Both Satake Shigeo and Sonobe Hideo became famous by their many victories in such contests.

These days, Jikishinkage-ryu no longer emphasizes competition against kendo practitioners, although they do still occur. Many members do participate in competitions in the modern, sports-oriented atarashi naginata (see below).

Jikishinkage-ryu is clearly a valued part of its practitioner's lives. Their main dojo appeared to be a place of joyous health and good spirits, full of both laughter and serious, finely honed practice. This seems in keeping with Jikishinkage-ryu's intention to create a system that will attract large numbers of women from many differing lifestyles. Jikishinkage-ryu has been more successful than any other martial system of the last one hundred years in appealing to a large population of Japanese women. In the forms of this system, they find a kind of semi-martial training that encourages the development of a strong, yet graceful femininity.

The Birth of Modern Competitive Martial Naginata-do

The Jikishinkage-ryu exemplifies a universalistic trend that grew in the Meiji period (1868-1912). As the Meiji progressed, the Japanese, ever increasingly, thought of themselves as having a national identity. Before the Meiji period, one's feudal domain was, in many senses, one's country.

The government began to rework the doctrines of bushido to make them apply to the entire populace rather than just the warrior class. Through this, the government encouraged the development of a regimented and obedient society. Language, religion, and education were brought under centralized control. The dogma of the day elevated the Emperor to the status of a god. Shinto was also perverted into a state religion, professing a pseudo-history that was used as a rationale for the 'manifest destiny' of Japan as the ruler of Asia. Following the same pattern of activities as the European and American imperialist powers, these sentiments carried the country through a war with Russia, the rape of northern China, and the horrors of World War II.

Used as a rallying point, this loyalty created an entire nation that was willing to live and die in the service of any cause deemed worthy by the government. The newly created grammar school system became a great propaganda machine. The primary emphases were on submission to the Emperor and gaining skills and knowledge for the good of the state. Students were taught that cooperation, standardization, and the denial of personal desires were the most productive ways of serving the nation.

Martial arts practice had been made a regular part of school curricula around the beginning of the 20th century. The classical disciplines, however, were not considered completely suitable for the training of the mass population. The older martial traditions encouraged a feudalistic loyalty to themselves and their teachings and, in addition, often focused on somewhat mystical values not directly concerned with the assumed needs of modern Japan. For this reason, judo and kendo, both Meiji creations, were taught in boys' schools. Kendo had been standardized by teachers of some of the major traditional systems of sword fighting for the purpose of specializing in competitive training. The length and weight of the shinai was fixed—rather longer than a real sword—and protective clothing was standardized. The head, sides of the trunk, the wrists, and a thrust to the throat became acceptable targets. All other strikes and thrusts, no matter how potentially lethal did not count for points.

Kendo developed from competitive practices with protective equipment called *uchiaigeiko* (striking-together practice) developed in the mid-Edo period in a number of different sword schools. This method became a relatively safe way to gauge each other's skills when compared to the only other alternatives: a duel, using wooden or edged weapons or a rather abstract evaluation of an individual's forms. Conservative martial artists, however, found this competitive style to be absurd. With safety equipment and body armor, one could take all sorts of 'risks' diving in to strike while allowing the edge of the opponent's 'weapon' to slide across the femoral artery or the back of the neck with no thought to the fatal injury one would suffer were one dueling with real weapons. Without the fear of either losing one's life or the dread of physical pain and injury, the conservatives felt that people moved unnaturally both in body and in spirit, becoming sportsmen rather than warriors. The innovative

"A match at the doio of Chiba Shusaku between naginata and shinai." Chiba Shusaku of the Hokushin Itto-ryu was one of the pioneers of competitive fighting/sports. *Photos courtesy of the Tokyo Central Library.*

practitioners felt, on the other hand, that in the absence of warfare or other conflict, kata training had degenerated into a sterile repetition of forms. Such innovators saw more conservative types as simply repeating a dull round of stereotypical movements that offered no means of testing the validity of their techniques, nor any insight into how they might perform with an opponent not colluding with them. As time passed, some ryu, such as the schools associated with Itto-ryu and Kashima Shinden Jikishinkage-ryu became famous for their strong practice using protective equipment. Others, such as Tenshinshoden Katori Shinto-ryu, never attempted to integrate this method into their practice.

There was another impetus for the development of competitive martial sports in the early Meiji period. This was the phenomenon of roving martial 'carnivals' known as *gekiken kogyo* (*gekiken* means 'attacking sword'; *kogyo* means 'show'). Former samurai, down on their luck, joined forces in traveling exhibitions, giving demonstrations and taking challenges from the audiences. Mounting the stage, fighters would challenge all comers from the audience, using wooden or bamboo swords, naginata, spear, chain-and-sickle, or any other weapon selected by the challenger. These fights were very popular and well written up in the newspapers. Although the fighters probably tried to exert some control, there were many injuries. In addition to challenge matches, members of the troop would engage each other in 'combat,' and among the most popular would be a woman with a wooden naginata against a man armed with a wooden or bamboo replica of a sword.

One of the most remarkable of these women was Murakami Hideo, who became the seventeenth-generation headmistress of Toda-ha Buko-ryu. The little that we know of her life-story cries for a novel in her name. She was born in Shikoku in 1863 and as a young girl studied Shizuga-ryu naginata-jutsu. When her teacher died, she moved to another area to study Ipponsai Ichiden-ryu. Still in her teens, she left her home and went to Kyushu, wandering from dojo to dojo. At one point, she studied a form of Shinkage-ryu. Then she continued her travels in Honshu, testing her skill against other fighters, studying as she went. Imagine a tiny, young woman, little more than a girl, marching through the Japanese countryside, alone, without employment, walking from one dojo to another. This was a time when women were severely restrained in their choice of lifestyle and employment, but Murakami went her own way, inviolate.

She reached Tokyo while in her early twenties and became a student of Komatsuzaki Koto, and, after her death, Yazawa Isao, fifteenth and sixteenth generation teachers of Toda-ha Buko-ryu. By now, Murakami was very strong.

and she was awarded a menkyo kaiden, at that time, the highest type of certification in the school, while still in her twenties. She opened a dojo in the Kanda area of Tokyo called the *Shusuikan* (Hall of Autumn Water).

Murakami was unable to read or write so, in a time when few in Japan had any interest in studying martial arts, all being swept away in a wave of modernization, she was not able to make a living. At some point, she joined the gekiken kogyo. Fighting with a kusarigama or naginata, she took all challenges from the audiences. There are no reports of her ever losing. In her later years, she was able to make ends meet as a teacher, but she was always poor. According to those who knew her in her old age, she was a tiny, kind, but wary women, always ready to invite you to supper. She could drink anyone under the table. As far as is known, she lived alone and she died alone.

As these matches were for the entertainment of a paying audience, they soon degenerated to what must be considered the pro-wrestling or 'Ultimate Fighting Championship' of the Meiji period, with the same level of vulgarity: waitresses serving drinks in abbreviated kimono and drunken patrons cheering in the stands. Matches became dramatic exhibitions, vulgar parodies of the austere warrior culture from which they had emerged. Discouraged by the police who regarded them as a threat to public order, the gekiken kogyo disbanded within a few years. Nonetheless, they can be regarded as the first precursors of modern martial sport in Japan—competition for the sake of comparing skills and entertaining an audience.

Murakami Hideo of the Toda-ha Buko-ryu with her successor, Kobayashi Seiko. Following photograph, they are teaching at a young girls' academy, probably in the mid-1930's. *Photos courtesy of the Kobayashi Family.*

Women's Martial Training in Modern Times

As martial arts continued to be integrated into public education during the first decades of the Showa period (1926 to 1989), the practice of naginata came to a crossroads. Judo, kendo, and, later, karate were made to be practiced in a standardized form. Naginata training, however, was still confined to the adaptation of specific ryu to physical education classes. Along with the Tendo-ryu's previously mentioned association with Doshisha's Girl's School, other prominent teachers also entered the education system. Yazawa Isao began teaching Toda-ha Buko-ryu at Nihon Joshi Daigaku in 1901, and Sonobe Hideo taught Jishinkage-ryu at Himeji Normal College, starting in 1908.[11] From these small beginnings, naginata instruction spread throughout the Japanese school systems, from junior high school through women's colleges. When taught to groups of young people, however, even the most traditional ryu must change. I have seen pre-Second World War photographs of a variety of koryu taught en masse, with lines of children diligently swinging weapons in unison.

Other pictures show young children phlegmatically plodding their way through kata. Form practice means something very different to warriors trying to get an edge in upcoming battles than it does to young teenagers attending gym class at the local high school. Therefore, competitive practice became more popular, not only as a means of training, but also as a way of holding the interest of young people who, understandably, could not see the value of kata practice alone. A light wooden naginata covered with leather was first used for competition; later, for safety, bamboo strips were attached to the end of a wooden shaft in imitation of kendo shinai. This replica weapon is light and whippy, allowing movements impossible with a real naginata. As rules developed and point targets were agreed upon, the techniques useful for victory in competition began to differ from those used by the old schools, each of which had been developed for different terrain and varied combative situations. Naginata practice began to develop into something new—a competitive sport.

Not all teachers were opposed to this universalistic trend, given its congruence with the strong centralization of state power at this time. During the Second World War, some naginata teachers, notably Sakakida Yaeko, in conjunction with the Ministry of Education created the *Monumbo Seiter Kata* (Standard Forms of the Ministry of Education). Sakakida was one of the senior practitioners of Tendoy-Ruy and was an avid competitor in navigant matches against kendo students. Nonetheless, she found that the sophisticated methods of the old Ruy were not suitable to teach to large groups of schoolgirls on an intermittent basis. She also believed that learning the sword side of kata, as was typical in most naginata kata, made things even more difficult, requiring the girls to learn a second weapon. Finally, she was concerned that they might study one ryu in primary school and another in secondary school, thus being required to relearn everything each time they switched schools.

She first began to emphasize solo practice with the naginata, but as one might imagine, this was not very popular with the girls. Therefore, she and several associates created totally new kata that focused upon the naginata against naginata. This combination is not unknown among koryu, but it is rather uncommon. Notable ryu that focus upon dual naginata practice include Toda-ha Buko-ryu, Higo Ko-ryu and Seiwa-ryu. Naginata instructors of traditions which emphasized the naginata against the sword could not, however, be forced to abandon their schools to enter one of the few, often obscure, traditions that had dual naginata forms. No one would imagine that teachers who had invested years, even decades, of training in one tradition would join another that was suddenly appointed the standard bearer by the state. Yet the needs of society and requirements of the state that dictated those needs seemed to require an efficient, simple method of teaching youth en masse. The Mombusho forms, made for the express purpose of training school children, were the result; they were adopted in 1943.

Something however, seems to have been lost in the process. Geared for children rather than warriors, these forms are, as a result, simplistic and

Murakami Hideo and Kobayashi Seiko teaching at a young girls' academy, probably in the mind-1930's.

somewhat lacking in character. The singularity that made the old ryu strong was sacrificed in favor of a generic mean. Teachers and students of the classical ryu received scant instruction in these new forms and were assigned 'territories' made up of several grammar schools. As part of their preparation, the teachers were instructed in how to give 'pep talks' to the girls. These talks included warnings about the barbarism of invading armies and the need for girls to protect themselves and their families. But the protection was not intended for the integrity of the girls themselves, but as "mirrors of the Emperor's virtue."[12]

Nitta Suzuyo, nineteenth-generation lineal successor to Toda-ha Buko-ryu recalled teaching these forms to girls from twelve to seventeen years old. Still a young woman herself, she was dispatched to instruct as her own teacher, Kobayashi Seiko, preferred to continue to teach her traditional ryu in private. As part of the training for teachers, Nitta was told that the most important thing was to boost the girls' morale and strengthen their spirit in case of an enemy landing. She said that the girls liked the training, which was done in place of 'enemy sports' such as baseball or volleyball.[13]

Women were said to personify the spirit of bushido because their nature was to be selfless and nurturing. They were believed to be the basis of society because of their place in the education of children. It was claimed that martial arts training would develop the attention to details needed for housekeeping, food preparation, caring for the sick, and making a 'friendly atmosphere.' A woman trained in naginata was supposed to be soft but strong, willing to be selfless but decisive, and above all, patient and enduring. The strong body she developed from training was necessary to keep healthy and active to carry out all her work. She was said to have a 'full spirit' and strong beauty. One teacher's manual, written in the middle of Japan's war years, states, "The study of naginata, home economics, and sewing will develop the perfect woman."[14]

In 1945, the war finally ended. The occupation forces were fearful of anything that seemed to be connected to Japan's warlike spirit and they banned public and institutional martial studies (private instruction was not, in fact, restricted). Thousands of swords were piled on runways, run over with steamrollers, and then buried under concrete construction projects. Noted martial arts practitioner and researcher Donn Draeger recounted to me the sight of those swords, flashing in the sun in shards of gold and silver, crackling and ringing under the roar and stink of the construction equipment.

In 1952, a group of senior martial artists, organized under the cover of the Japan National Health Association and chaired by Prince Tsunenori Kaya (an uncle of Emperor Hirohito and a former lieutenant-general in the Imperial Army), held the first large-scale, public martial arts demonstration during the Occupation in Hibiya Park in downtown Tokyo. Quickly following this, the International Martial Arts Federation (IMAF) was established, and chaired by another of the Emperor's uncles, Prince Higashikuni, the first post Second World War prime minister. Soon afterwards, all bans were lifted, and martial arts training resumed in schools throughout Japan.[15]

The first *Zen Nihon Kendo Renmei* (All Japan Kendo Federation) Tournament was held in 1953. At a meeting held afterwards, Sakakida and several of the leading naginata instructors of Tendo-ryu and Jikishinkage-ryu made plans for the institution of a similar *Zen Nihon Naginata-do Renmei* (All Japan Naginata Federation). It was decided to adopt the Mombusho kata as the standard form of the federation, with only a few minor changes. They also decided to eliminate the writing of naginata in characters (長刀 – long blade) or (薙刀 – reaping blade) and, to indicate their break with the past, spell it in the syllabary, whose letters have only sound values. This martial sport has come to be called *atarashi naginata* (あたらしいなぎなた 'new naginata').

The change of characters in writing naginata may seem to be a trivial one, but it is not. The philosopher Maurice Merleau-Ponty refers to language as 'sublimated flesh.' By this, he means that language is the concentrated essence of human existence and determines how life will be lived. This change implicitly states that atarashi naginata is no longer a martial art, using a weapon either to train combat skills, or to demand, through its paradoxical claim as a 'tool for enlightenment,' a focused and integrated spirit. Instead, they have created a sports form, martial in both appearance and 'sound,' but not in 'character.'

Atarashi naginata is composed of two parts: kata and shiai. According to some of its leading instructors, particularly those of this generation, the kata were created by taking "the best techniques from many naginata ryu." Perhaps some may feel that I am stating this a little too strongly, but this is an absurd idea. The forms of the various ryu are not mere catalogues of separate techniques to be selected like bon-bons in a corner candy store. They are interrelated systems, permeated with a sophisticated cultivation of movement, for combative effectiveness and/or spiritual training. Sakakida herself only states that she observed the old ryu and tried to absorb their essence. Then, forgetting their movements entirely, she devised the new kata.

Atarashii naginata forms competition.
Photo courtesy of E. Amdur.

These first-level kata, derived from the Mombusho forms and now called *shikake-oji*, are a set of simple movements requiring straight posture and sliding footwork. Practice is done with an extremely light shinai or wooden naginata.

These forms are used in kata contests. Two pairs of contestants perform the same kata, and they are judged on the 'correctness' of their movements. There is a second level of forms, called the *Zen Nihon Naginata Kata*, which is only taught after a student reaches third dan level. Some claim that they are the product of a study of the naginata kata from fifteen different martial traditions. A committee of members of the *Zen Nihon Naginata-do Renmei* allegedly derived what they considered to be the essential movements of these ryu and combined them into a linked set of seven kata. However, according to martial arts scholar Meik Skoss, the forms are, in fact, largely comprised of techniques from Tendo-ryu and Jikishinkage-ryu.

Not all of the old teachers are enamored of atarashi naginata. Abe Toyoko, a senior instructor of Tendo-ryu, in a marvelous interview in *Fighting Woman News* discussed these forms with Kini Collins in the early 1980s. Abe Sensei was one of the strongest of all the powerful women in Tendo-ryu and had always been rather a lone wolf. Japanese social groups can be rather wearing, and Abe Sensei was well known for her blunt speech and strong opinions. Her almost gruff power was reflected in her art and her words. The first time I saw her in a group of other Tendo-ryu instructors, she stood out like a mother bear. She never seemed to try to look pretty or graceful—simply effective. She said:

Abe Toyoko of the Tendo-ryu explaining how to lock an opponent's elbow, immobilizing him so that he cannot escape as he is stabbed with a short weapon. *Photo courtesy of E. Amdur.*

This new stuff! One, up with the stick. Two, down with it. Three, put it away. Well, that is one way of teaching, but there is something else, I only know it as *kokoro* (heart, spirit). Pull it in on one, out on two, lift on three, well, you try it! If you do it only with an awareness of moving and no concept of kokoro, you are so wide open it isn't even funny. This is what I want to teach. How to react when your partner doesn't respond in the way you are used to. This is what it hasn't got, the new naginata. There is no thought outside the form; there isn't even any path for this kind of thinking.

When they got started about twenty years ago, they wanted to get going fast, so it was forced: trying to bring everyone into the same line, changing everyone's style to fit a new form. Taking from the right, from the left, trying to get everyone to agree. Just to get started, never mind the outcome. But all these schools and the techniques themselves are separate entities governed by separate principles of movement and thought. This new thing has absolutely none of these principles.

Teaching the form of a technique rather than the substance and form leads to nothing. Worse than nothing. Some teachers say that form is enough for women. No way! That really makes me angry. Who needs form? In Japanese, there is a word, *rashikute* (to seem or to be like something), like a woman, like a man, like a …I don't know what, but it really colors our language. It has meaning though, not just the surface stereotypes. A woman's whole life is being womanlike. To be like a woman is not simply to be soft. To be womanlike is to be as strong or as soft, as servile or as demanding as a situation calls for. Be appropriate and act with integrity. This isn't being taught at all. And it is the heart of budo; it is alive in the practice of it.[16]

The atarashii naginata competitions are an imitation of those of kendo. Sadly, the matches often resemble a game of tag with the naginata shinai. It is remarkable to see how few techniques in the kata movements the practitioners in shiai utilize. The kata, are thus, in many ways, not relevant to the other wing of the system

The contestants are well armored, but there are only eight designated targets: the top of the wrists, the top and sides of the head, the throat, the sides of the trunk, and the shins. Referees decide winning points. Considering that the bamboo end of the shinai is supposed to represent the blade of the naginata, the contests are often a little confusing for outsiders. Many potentially lethal or incapacitating strikes go unheeded because they do not represent a 'point.' In addition, the *ishizuki* (butt-end) of the shinai is rarely used in such competitions, although it was an essential component of the use of the weapon in real combat. Because one scores by striking target areas with an extremely light replica of a weapon, the emphasis is on speed. The contestants hold their bodies upright on the balls of their feet to slide and jump in and out quickly, footwork suited only to the polished floors of gymnasiums and dojo.

Modern naginata competition. The weight is high, on the balls of the feet. The opponent's spar, looking for an opening to dart in and strike. *Photo courtesy of E. Amdur.*

Because there is no sense of danger or even a need to protect undesignated targets, many competitors do not move or respond in a natural way. Blows that would sever arms, disfigure, or even kill are ignored because they are not designated targets. Again, consider the words of Abe Toyoko:

> Our matches didn't have all that quick jumping and dancing. They never did. There has to be a lot of awareness before and during a match. You can't just enter one casually. Naginata were weapons with blades that cut, and we have to keep that respect even with the bamboo blades we use today. The first tournament I saw my teacher in, it was amazing. She walked her opponent all the way across the hall, from the east side to the west side, not using any technique, just her stance and spirit. Everyone, even the old teachers were enthralled. Then she moved to cut, just once. And I was hooked. She found my timing and caught me. She won the match too.[17]

By removing the considerations of one's own death and one's responsibility for the other's fate, atarashi naginata may have removed one of the major impetuses for the development of an ethical stance. All that may remain for many trainees is a sport with the emphasis on wining or losing a match.

Many naginata-ryu teachers have entered the modern association and have attempted to teach both their own traditions as well as atarashi naginata. However, only a few of their students are willing to practice the old ryu. These martial traditions, with footwork suited to rough terrain and low postures suited to exerting leverage in cutting and protecting all of the body, seem to be awkward and old fashioned to atarashi naginata students who focus on modern competition. This has resulted in the abandonment and demise of most of the old martial traditions within the last fifty years. Often the only reason young people practice the old school at all is "just so it won't be forgotten."

When searching out old schools, it was disheartening to see how many schools that had made common cause with atarashi naginata, rather than getting new students, ended up with none. I've been informed that most Tendo-ryu instructors only begin teaching their own tradition *after* their students have achieve third dan or higher in atarashii naginata. From one perspective, this could make sense—sportive practice can develop a fighting spirit, endurance, timing and physical strength. However, by that time, one's nervous system is permeated by the 'movement signature' of atarashii naginata, one that is, as I have discussed, profoundly at variance with that of any classical

The magnificent **Sakurada Tomi**, eighteenth-generation headmistress of the Suzuga-ryu, without a successor, demonstrating alone. *Photos courtesy of E. Amdur.*

ryu. I am not alone in this criticism. Mabuchi Seiko, surely the finest practitioner of Tendo-ryu in this generation, adamantly refuses to dilute her Tendo-ryu with the modern sportive form. Mabuchi Sensei's Tendo-ryu is powerful and intimidating, hearkening back to the age of Mitamura Kengyo and Mitamura Chiyo. Unlike the stylized practice of most other teachers, one could well envision her walking an opponent across the length of a dojo floor, unable to retaliate, captured by will and intensity alone.

In the early 1980s, it took three months of concentrated effort to locate Sakurada Tomi, the eighteenth-generation headmistress of the Suzuka-ryu, one of the foremost naginata instructors in Japan, the last headmistress of her tradition. Numerous calls to both the local and national offices of the Atarashi Naginata Association were met with indifference, although she had been perhaps the most significant figure among women martial artists in Sendai city. We finally located her, alone, without students or family.

With the 'official line' trivializing the classical schools to young impressionable students, the older ryu, with the exception of Tendo-ryu and Jikishinkage-ryu, are largely ignored, except to be invited to give demonstrations at the intermissions of atarashi naginata competitions. Among the traditions that have almost or completely died out in the last twenty years, we must number Chokugen-ryu, with its massive nine-foot-long naginata, the vital and powerful Suzuka-ryu and elegant Anazawa-ryu. The dynamic Muhen-ryu, a school that interestingly uses naginata and *bo* (long-staff) interchangeably within the same forms, is also largely ignored by the atarashi naginata students who study under its headmistress.

Muhen-ryu Naginata. In this unusual form, called "Rat Hole," the naginata is rested on the shoulders then suddenly snapped around the body and forward with a springing action. If the swordfighter is not exceptionally quick, his lead leg will be severed. *Photos courtesy of the Nippon Budokan.*

It must be faced, however, that much of the demise of the old traditions is the responsibility of practitioners themselves, who either could not find a way to make their art relevant to the younger generation, or have no idea themselves of the value of the tradition passed on to them. Illustrative of the latter was one woman, an atarashi naginata competitor and teacher who had practiced a bujutsu ryu since childhood.

I said to her, "Your training in classical naginata must give you a real advantage in strength over the other participants in contests."

In response, she complained, "No matter what I do, the naginata-jutsu techniques creep into my atarashi naginata movements and ruin it. We are all supposed to do it the same way, but I just can't!"

This attitude, too, is countered by Abe Toyoko:

> I see lots of people today, jumping from one new thing to another, not getting settled. I really think people need something in the foundation, some deeply rooted place in their lives. I see this even in the judging of naginata matches. It used to be so different, this judging. There were only two judges per match, and they were deliberate and subtle, not jumpy and conforming like the ones today. Even their movements had more meaning. The judges used to have individual styles, their own way of signaling points. Now everyone has to do it

the same way. You won't believe this. They stopped a match once, one I was judging, and asked over the loudspeaker if I would raise my arm a few more degrees when signaling. Do you believe it? And just a couple of years ago, I was judging with another teacher. One of the competitors moved, just moved a little, and the other judge signaled a point. I asked the two women in the match if a point had been made, and they both said no. But because the judge had ruled for it, it was declared valid! I haven't judged since. I don't want to participate in teaching people how to win cheaply or lose unfairly.[18]

Conclusion

From an essay in history sprinkled with only minor leavenings of personal opinion, I find it necessary to end on a truly personal note. Approximately thirty-five years ago, I began a project on the use and history of the naginata. The initial stages of this were done in the company of Ms. Kini Collins: I later took the project over by myself, and a series of essays became a book: *Old School: Essays on Japanese Martial Traditions* (2014).

This weapon attracted me the first time I saw it, not as a 'woman's weapon,' but one suited for me, a man of six and a half feet and over 230 pounds (105 kilos). Araki-ryu, the first martial tradition I enrolled, uses both the nagamaki and a large naginata in a ferocious, almost wild fashion probably very similar to the methods of strapping foot soldiers and warrior monks in earlier periods of Japanese history.

I later entered Toda-ha Buko-ryu, and, thereafter, was able to study a system that, until the ascension of its 20th generation headmaster, Nakamura Yoichi, and his successor, sokedairi, Kent Sorensen, had been led by women for over one hundred and fifty years. Toda-ha Buko-ryu is still very much an art of war, but it is a martial tradition that developed and permutated in the Edo period. It is a paradoxical art—every movement is an attack. There is no stance with the weight on the back foot, and no purely defensive techniques. Yet in its elegant, graceful movements, it shows some of the sophistication that develops in a martial art when warriors have the leisure afforded them by peace to study movement and refine it in depth. It is also imbued, for lack of a better term, with a profound feminine sensibility.

I became deeply influenced by both of these martial traditions, both in themselves and as embodied in the person of their instructors. Of most relevance to this piece is Nitta Suzuyo, 19th generation headmistress of Toda-ha Buko-ryu, a refined, gracious woman, unfailingly courteous and remarkably strong in every sense that really matters. The feminine leadership within this school was a gift and a challenge to me. I was required to template myself, in some respects, on a tiny, five-foot-tall, aristocratic Japanese woman, to learn the essence of what she offered without either slavish imitation or an arrogant assumption on my part that I could simply adapt her art to my large, Western frame. She was a model to me in my own profession dealing with the diffusion and de-escalation of violence. It was from her that I learned the power of tact, how courtesy alone can often resolve what force of arms may not.

I have, therefore, an intense attachment and respect for the traditional koryu and firmly believe that the best of my own life's work could never have occurred without my study in them. It is fair to say that there have been instances in which I have been able to save people's lives using knowledge that I could have acquired in no other fashion than by training in archaic Japanese martial arts, and in none of these instances was I forced to engage in anything like hand-to-hand combat.

I believe that competitive martial sports can be wonderful activities as well. My own rather limited years of experience in judo, Muay Thai and Brazilian jiujitsu have certainly brought that home to me. Competition can impart a sense of trust in one's ability as well as expose one's weaknesses. Such study can create a more self-aware individual, a person far more valuable to a community than one would imagine a mere sportswoman or sportsman to be. Martial sports are not *merely* sports.

Atarashi naginata is a significant part of the lives of probably several million women. Something of such consequence cannot simply be shoved aside in a disdainful conservative critique that it is degenerated, watered-down martial arts. Like any other activity, martial training must continue to grow and develop if it is to remain appropriate to the times in which it exists.

However, in the rush to create martial sports that are open to anyone and useful to everyone, much of profound value is irrevocably lost. Tradition, far from being a mere nostalgia for the past, can be a powerful force to unite a people. Traditions can make people aware of their origins and singularity. Even though martial ryu were created hundreds of years ago to deal with problems specific to those times, there is no reason to relegate them to preservation societies or museums, mere curiosities to be trotted out several times a year as intermission entertainment during competitive matches. Since the ryu were developed for specific regions, offering specific psychological and combative methods, they can still be living traditions, strong and direct connections with the past. They were, and can be, powerful forces imparting loyalty, morality, and courage, as well as a sense of togetherness. That which helped create viable communities in the Muromachi era is still relevant today. Practiced with the

Nitta Suzuyo nineteenth-generation headmistress of the Toda-ha Buko-ryu.
Photo courtesy of E. Amdur.

intention of strengthening its community, study of any ryu can develop a cohesive courage and depth of feeling in its members. This could help maintain a community as a living entity, one not as vulnerable to exploitation or incorporation into a superficial mass culture.

Finally, the knowledge contained in the ryu was bought in blood. I do not idealize the act of killing on a battlefield. I do idolize those who passed through such experiences and, rather than leaving mere reminiscences of brutal acts committed or suffered, attempted to pass on a treasure distilled from the horrors of war: the knowledge of how to survive; a method of continuing the bonding that occurs on the battlefield well after the battle was fought, maintaining those ties of trust once the shackles of fear and rage are no longer needed to force people together; and perhaps most important, a tradition for handing on the depths of ethical and spiritual teachings contained in the heart of systems created ostensibly only for war. On my own father's gravestone are the words of Rabbi Hillel, "In a land where there are no men, strive thou to be a man." This is morality learned on the battlefield, however the battlefield might be defined. This is an ethic won only through facing the potential for death: one's own at the hands of others and others' death at our own hands. To strive towards this ethical sense is what has led me through my over forty-five of martial training, and this is, to me, the essence of what is contained in the heart of many of the traditional ryu. For the men and women in most modern martial sports, and, specifically, for the (mostly) women who train in modern sports naginata, I believe that despite all the fine things they may have gained in the abandonment of traditional martial practice, they may have lost even more wondrous things. To wish that history were different is ultimately foolish. But foolish as it may be, I wish that they could have both.

Notes

1. McCullough, Helen Craig, trans., *The Tale of the Heike*, Stanford University Press, California, 1988. (For this and all further references to Tomoe Gozen.)
2. http://todahaBukoryu.org/wp/wp-content/uploads/2010/07/Yazawa-Isao-writings.pdf
3. In a book published in the early 1970s, a master instructor of the Takenouchi-ryu writes that the women of the Takenouchi family trained with naginata and learned self-defense when they were young. As adults, they were "...very busy taking care of the house and had little time to practice. However, when bringing tea to the dojo for the male students, they had an opportunity to listen to the teacher's instructions and pick up some of the movements that they saw being practiced" from Takenouchi-ryu Hensan I-in Kai, Takenouchi-ryu, p. 104
4. Statistics from a 1764 inspection of a feudal domain in what is now modern-day Okayama show that the castle had 3,787 muskets and its retainers, another 4,698 muskets and 1,265 hunting guns. Three thousand three hundred and sixteen spears were kept at the castle and another 5,010 distributed among the retainers. Only fifty naginata were counted in this survey. As in footnote #36, my apologies to those concerned with historical and textual accuracy. I recorded this quote from a Japanese language source some thirty years ago, but no longer have the citation.
5. http://en.wikipedia.org/wiki/Nakano_Takeko
6. http://aamatsushima.blogspot.com/2013/03/biographical-spotlight-nakano-takeko.html
7. Shimazu, ibid.
8. Shimazu, Masayoshi, "The Battle of Aizu," http://www.bakumatsu.ru/lib/Shimazu_Masayoshi_The_Battle_of_Aizu.pdf
9. For more on this remarkable woman, one can start with this Wikipedia article and branch out from there http://en.wikipedia.org/wiki/Yamamoto_Yaeko.
10. Larry Bieri, martial arts scholar and long-time student of Tendo-ryu,

informed me that the old Tendo-ryu naginata was tapered, getting progressively wider at the butt end for better balance and a stronger grip. This practical design is no longer included in modern-day Tendo-ryu practice naginata.

[11] Bennett, Alex, in *Martial Arts of the World: An Encyclopedia of History and Innovation*, ed. By Green, Thomas, and Svinth, Joseph, ABO-CLIO, LLC, Santa Barbara, California, 2010, p. 160.

[12] Sonobe, Shigehachi, *Kokumin Gakko Naginata Seigi*, page 7.

[13] Personal communication with Nitta Suzuyo.

[14] Ibid, page 7.

[15] A shibboleth, which I, among many, have subscribed to, states that all martial arts were banned. This was not, in fact, true, as established by the research of Dr. Yamamoto Reiko and others, translated and expanded by Lance Gatling. The passage above is a personal communication from Mr. Gatling.

[16] This, and all subsequent quotes of Abe Sensei were published in the early 1980s by Ms. Kini Collins in "Fighting Woman News." The author and Ms. Collins were working on a project regarding the history of the naginata, and this interview was one of its aspects. With Ms. Collins permission, I have retained the original manuscript for this interview and have made some very minor changes in syntax for ease in reading. The meaning has not been changed in any respect.

[17] Ibid.

[18] Ob cit.

Bibliography
English Language Sources

Amdur, E. (1994a). Divine transmission katori shinto ryu. *Journal of Asian Martial Arts*, 3:2, 48-61.

Amdur, E. (1994b). The higo ko ryu. *Furyu*, 1:3, 49-54.

Amdur, E. (1995a). The development and history of the naginata. *Journal of Asian Martial Arts*, 4:1, 32-49.

Amdur, E. (1995b). The rise of the curved blade. *Furyu*, 1:4, 58-68.

Amdur, E. (1995c). Maniwa nen-ryu. *Journal of Asian Martial Arts*, 4:3, 10-25.

Dore, R. P. (1965). *Education in Tokugawa Japan*. London: Routlege and Kegan Paul.

Draeger, D., & Smith, R. (1969). *Asian fighting arts*. Tokyo: Kodansha, Ltd.

Frederic, L. (1973). *Daily life at the time of the samurai 1185-1603* (E. Lowe, Trans.). Tokyo: Charles E. Tuttle Co.

Mason, P. (1977). *A reconstruction of the hogen-heiji monogatari emaki*. New York: Garland Pub., Inc.

McCullough, H. C. (Trans.). (1966). *Yoshitsune*. Tokyo: University of Tokyo Press.

McCullough, H. C. (Trans.). (1979). *Taiheiki*. Tokyo: Charles E. Tuttle Co.

Sadler, A. L. (Trans.). (1941). *Heike monogatari*. Tokyo: Kimiwada Shoten.

Varley, P. (1994). *Warriors of Japan as portrayed in the war tales*. Honolulu, HI: University of Hawaii Press.

Wilson, W. (Trans.). (1971). *Hogen monogatari*. Tokyo: Sophia University Press.

Japanese Language Sources

Mitamura, Kunihiko. (1939). *Dai Nippon naginata-do kyoden*. Tokyo: Shubundo Shoten. [Prewar school instructor's book for Tendo-ryu].

Kendo Nippon Monthly. (1982). "Naginata: Interview with Sakakida Yaeko." *Kendo Nippon Monthly*, No. 7.

Sonobe, Shigehachi. (1941). *Kokumin gakko naginata seigi*. Tokyo: Toytosho Pub. [Prewar school instructor's book for Jikishinkage-ryu].

Takenouchi-ryu hensan i-in kai. (1979). *Takenouchi-ryu*. Tokyo: Nochibo-Shuppan Sha. [Large book detailing the history and techniques of the Takenouchi-ryu].

Yazawa, Isako. (1916). *Naginata no hanashi*. [In a collection of martial arts articles held by the Toda-ha Buko-ryu].

NOTE

This chapter has been updated since it was originally published in the *Journal of Asian Martial Arts*. Thanks to author Ellis Amdur and Gregory Mele, publisher of the 2nd expanded edition of the *Old School: Essays on Japanese Martial Traditions* (2014). See: www.freelanceacademypress.com

· 2 ·

Martial-Acrobatic Arts in Peking Opera With a Brief Analysis of Fighting Movement in a Scene from *The Three-Forked Crossroad*

by Yao Haihsing, Ph.D.

In Peking Opera, actor Zhu Luhao is famous for his roles playing a general with superb fighting skills. *Photo courtesy of the National Kuo-kuang Chinese Opera Company in Taiwan. Lee Minghsun, photographer. All photos courtesy of Yao Haihsing, except where noted.*

Introduction

Fighting movement is perhaps the most fascinating element of Peking Opera performance. Particularly in military plays, warriors and soldiers perform flips, jumps, turns, combat with weapons, and other fairly difficult movements on the stage, producing effects that are visually striking and aesthetically pleasing. It is difficult for us not to be touched by the actors' neat and nimble movements. Peking Opera is often regarded as a type of musical theater, but we must not forget that it is also a highly physical theater.

It is necessary first to define the term "martial-acrobatic arts" used in this article. In Peking Opera, movements frequently seen in fighting scenes of military plays can be classified into two distinct types: the acrobatics and the martial arts (Mackerras, 1983: 132-33; Yao, 1990: 19-28). The former primarily refers to tumbling, such as somersaults or cartwheels; the latter alludes to the arts of self-defense, including both unarmed and armed combat. In some of the English-written materials that deal with Peking Opera, the fighting movements are called acrobatics or fighting arts (or martial arts). Unfortunately, neither term can embrace both types of movements that appear in opera performance. In Chinese, these movements are termed *wugong*, which refers to both acrobatics and martial arts. To make the connotation of the word precise, wugong is translated as "martial-acrobatic arts," to indicate the uniting of two different systems: the acrobatics and the martial arts.

Although martial-acrobatic arts are a fascinating performance element, scholars have not been studied them much. There is still a great deal we need to know about these arts. In old China, wugong arts were often viewed as an insignificant vaudeville type of craft by theatergoers whereas spectators highly appreciated plays dominated by singing, which was regarded as a superior and more refined element. Perhaps this traditional attitude toward martial-acrobatic arts has led to the limited research in this field.

While it is true that most martial-acrobatic movements in Peking Opera were arranged and choreographed by various master actors rather than by intellectuals, that does not mean those movements were merely a type of vaudeville used to create spectacular effects. In fact, the martial-acrobatic arts are a much more important performance element than we think, and they are intimately integrated with acting. This chapter intends to explore the significance of these arts and the different layers of meaning they represent in Peking Opera.

Armed and ready for battle, Zhu Luhao (left) smiles as he faces Li Xiaoping. *Photo courtesy of the National Kuo-kuang Chinese Opera Company in Taiwan. Lee Minghsun, photographer.*

A Means of Developing a Healthy Body and a Strong Will

Chinese martial arts have unbroken traditions that go back thousands of years. In ancient times, people practiced martial arts for various purposes, with one of the major ones being to improve their physical health. As martial arts gradually developed through the centuries, health improvement has remained an important goal. A good example is taijiquan; by practicing it, many practitioners believe that their health may be improved. As a matter of fact, nearly all Chinese martial arts have a similar function.

After martial-acrobatic arts became a performance element of Peking Opera, the actors who practiced the arts still believed in the idea of developing a healthy body and a strong will. In fact, good health is an extremely important requirement of a Peking Opera actor, especially a fighting actor, and continuously practicing the martial-acrobatic arts is a way to improve his health.

It has been a tradition that fighting actors must practice martial-acrobatic arts in the early morning. In the past, they were required by their mentors to practice before daybreak. Famous fighting actor Gai Jiaotian said that when he was a child, his wugong practice began before dawn (Hebeisheng, 1986: 10-11). Actress Guan Sushuang also said that in her childhood her daily practice started very early in the morning when the stars were still in the sky (Guan, 1979: 40). This habit of getting up early to practice continues today. For example, the students of the Fuxing Peking Opera School in Taiwan[1] are required to practice acrobatics at 6 a.m. daily (Yao, 1990: 112). Actress Chang Xiangyu believes that getting up early to drill the martial-acrobatic exercises makes an actor healthy (Chang, 1981, May: 53). She points out that in the early morning, the air is fresh as are the actor's body and mind; therefore, it is very beneficial to exercise at that time of day (Chang, 1981, February: 58). If an actor rises early everyday to practice, then his daily schedule requires him to establish a routine, which is not only good for his health, but also helps him develop discipline as an actor. Sun Xing observes that an actor's physical condition should be excellent after insisting on continuously doing daily martial-acrobatic exercises for many years (Sun, 1980: 4).

But why is a healthy, strong body so important to a fighting actor? On the one hand, the martial-acrobatic movements are fast, powerful, and very demanding. The actor is easily drained of energy performing these movements alone; but, on the stage, he is required to perform these difficult movements and at the same time acting in a relaxed manner. On the other hand, the actor's costume is heavy. Although some of the fighting roles, such as bandits or outlaws, may wear lighter outfits, the actor who portrays a general or a warrior is required to wear a fairly heavy headpiece plus a thick, heavy, but loose garment (*kao*, meaning "armor"). A Western dancer may perform with a more fitted costume made of light and thin materials, which makes it easier for him to move. But a Peking Opera fighting actor's task is much more difficult. When wearing a thick, heavy garment and headpiece, the actor is often very uncomfortable and breathless, but he still needs to perform fast combat movements and sometimes jump, turn, and flip (Zhu, 1990). Therefore, a healthy, strong body is definitely, an indispensable tool for a fighting actor. Without a strong, energetic body an actor quickly feels exhausted and breathless after performing martial-acrobatic movements for a moment, not to mention the fact that he has to sustain a performance for one or two hours.

Besides a strong body, a strong will is also essential for the actor and the practice of the martial arts helps enhance will power (Xi, et al., 1984: 5, 8, 10). The long and difficult training period requires the practitioner to have a strong will.

There are four basic skills of a Peking Opera actor: singing, acting, speech delivery, and fighting. An opera actor's training includes all four aspects, each of which is very demanding. To learn all the skills, the training period is very long. For instance, at the Fuxing Peking Opera School, a student needs to train for eight years before he can graduate. A fighting actor's training is particularly tiring (Yao, 1990a: 160-162). Though not all the fighting roles require the actor to master all four skills, many fighting roles do. It is an exhausting process to perfect scenes in which the actor must present acting, singing, and martial-acrobatic movements at the same time. Without a strong will, the fighting actor could not possibly sustain this long and painful process (Zhu, 1990), and he would soon want to give up his career. Even the actor of civil plays needs a strong will, which supports him through the difficult process of learning the roles of heavy singing and complicated postures.

The actor's will power may be enhanced through the practice of martial-acrobatic arts. The rigid discipline of wugong training tests the actor's will power, because the endless repetition of the martial-acrobatic movements is extremely tedious and tiring. Moreover, many basic wugong exercises demand great perseverance. They require the actor to hold a still pose for a period of time (*hao*). For instance, when practicing the *nading* (handstand), the actor is required to keep the upside-down pose for at least several minutes without moving. Sometimes a more rigorous mentor will demand his pupils to keep the posture a lot longer. Another example is the *shanbang*, which is an exercise for the arms. The actor stands straight, raises both arms horizontally to shoulder level, and lets each arm form a slight curve. The exercises mentioned above are not difficult, but stillness is the basic requirement for all those exercises.

The *shanbang* exercise for the arms.

To keep the body still in a specific posture for a period of time can be very uncomfortable, or even unbearable, because the muscles soon become sore. At this point, the actor must rely on his will power to sustain his pose, gradually strengthening his will power after continuously practicing these exercises for some time. In short, for many years, actors have regarded martial-acrobatic arts as useful physical exercises for developing a strong, healthy body and a strong will, which are an actor's most basic requirements.

A Basic Physical Training for an Actor

Physical training is essential for a Peking Opera performer. Fighting is often considered the most basic of the four basic skills. Because physical techniques are frequently required in performance, it is essential for an actor to know them. Sun Xing points out that even an actor who specializes in civil plays is required to be a skillful practitioner of martial-acrobatic arts. With martial-acrobatic training, the actor's stage movements will be much lighter, swifter, and more precise than that of an actor without such training (Sun, 1980: 2). Famous fighting actor Wang Jinlu also believes that martial-acrobatic arts are essential for an actor. He observes that even a supernumerary should not avoid practicing these arts because good training in such arts enables him to perfect simple physical movements, such as standing or running on the stage (Wang, 1983: 62).

In fact, it became a tradition that Peking Opera school or private opera teachers in old China always requested beginning students to practice these arts no matter what role types they were going to focus on in the future. This was to provide the students solid physical training and to build their capability for a wider range of roles, both non-fighting and fighting (Liu, 1980: 432). For example, at the Conservatory of Dramatic Art, a Peking Opera school founded in 1930, all beginning students were required to go through the basic training of martial-acrobatic movements without considering their later area of specialization (Mackerras, 1983: 121-122). Many famous Peking Opera actors received excellent martial-acrobatic training in their early childhoods. Mei Lanfang reminisced in his memoirs that he rigorously trained in martial-acrobatic arts in his youth (Mei, 1957: 33-34). Cheng Yanqiu, a famous actor of *qingyi* roles,[2] also had solid training in these arts when he was very young. When he grew older, he even studied martial arts, which had a significant influence on his art (Cheng, 1981: 37, 40, 43).

This tradition of regarding martial-acrobatic arts as an actor's basic physical training continues into the present. At the Fuxing Peking Opera School, the martial-acrobatic arts are still considered the most basic curriculum; beginning students are required to devote their mornings to the practice of these arts for at least two years (Yao, 1990a: 112).

Zhu Luhao (left, wearing a white outfit) in a fight scene with Tang Wenhua. *Photo courtesy of the National Kuo-kuang Chinese Opera Company in Taiwan. Lee Minghsun, photographer.*

But why did the master teachers in the past insist on using the martial-acrobatic arts to train their actors? It is because these arts can be used as effective exercises for developing the actor's physical movement. A well-trained body is very necessary to an actor.

> A good, well-functioning body is not enough; it must be an "understanding" one that can respond readily to an idea or a situation with flexibility, sensitivity, profundity and assurance. The actor must be capable of a wide range of expressive "textures," and he must be in control of body changes and adjustments.
> – Delza, 1972: 28

A free, expressive and spontaneous body is particularly necessary for a Peking Opera actor because of the numerous bodily postures and combat movements required by the roles, and the martial-acrobatic arts are especially helpful for training a body of this kind. Richard Nichols said:

> All the martial arts lead to physical development and a greater kinesthetic sense of surrounding space.... The martial arts, with their emphasis on mind-body balance and unity, can be most helpful in the greater integration of the actor, awakening right brain potential while developing greater physical awareness.
> – Nichols, 1991: 53

The martial-acrobatic arts are very useful for developing four physical elements. The first is flexibility. A flexible body is essential for an acrobatics performer. Martial-acrobatic training greatly emphasizes the development of flexibility in the waist and legs (Wang, et al., 1982: 9). There are many exercises to improve flexibility. For example, the *chaotian deng* (vertical leg stretching), which requires the actor to stand on one leg and raise the other leg vertically, and the *pitui* (splits) are the basic leg exercises; the back bend and the forward and the backward walkover are the basic waist exercises. With flexible legs and a flexible waist, the actor can do perfect flips and turns (Yao, 1990a: 151).

The second physical element is muscle strength. The training stresses the development of both arm and leg muscles. Many acrobatic movements depend on the arms to support the body. Without strong muscles, the arms are not able to carry the body weight. Exercises such as the handstand and weapon manipulation are especially effective for strengthening arm muscles. The development of leg muscles relies more on martial-type exercises; for example, the *aibu* (crouched walk), which requires the actor to crouch down with his back straight and walk forward, and the *titui* (leg kicking) are good exercises to build strong leg muscles. Without strong legs, it is impossible to perform the powerful kicks used in some of the advanced martial exercises.

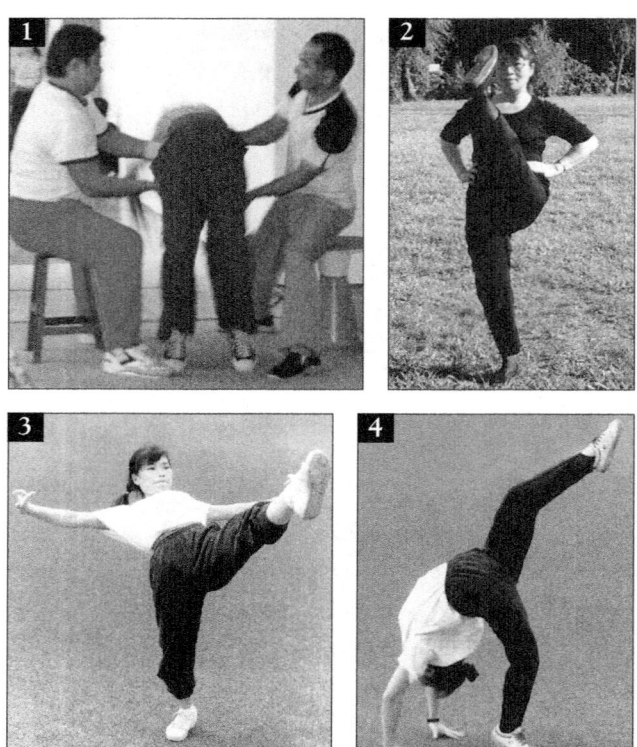

1) Two teachers helping a student to learn the back bend. 2) *Titui* leg kicking exercise. 3) The *sheyan*, a typical exercise for balance. 4) The backward walkover.

    The third physical element is balance. A number of martial-type exercises demand a practitioner be able to balance his body immediately and remain still after quick jumps and turns (Xi, 1984: 28). The *sheyan* (upward balance movement) is a typical balance exercise. It requires the actor to lean backward with arms open and raise one leg; the raised leg and the upper part of the body form a nearly horizontal line. The actor should hold this pose for a while. The ability to balance his body enables the actor to perform much more clear-cut and precise movements.

    The fourth physical element is control. A large part of martial-acrobatic exercises involve flips and turns. An example is the *danmanzi* (aerial cartwheel), which is a cartwheel without the hands touching the floor. It is essential that the actor have good coordination and control of his body when he performs difficult stunts such as the aerial cartwheel, otherwise he gets injured. The continuous practice of these exercises enhances his ability to control his body for any desired movements.

Basic exercises for weapon manipulation are very helpful for strengthening the arm muscles.

As we can see, the martial-acrobatic arts have long been used as effective exercises for physical training. Almost every actor, even a supernumerary, must receive solid training in these arts. The result is the development of a flexible and spontaneous body that can be manipulated freely. That is why actor Wang Jinlu observes that without fundamental martial-acrobatic training one cannot possibly become a Peking Opera actor (Wang, 1983: 62).

A Type of Dance Form

Although the martial arts may be taken as exercises for improving health, they are essentially self-defense methods. Over the centuries, they have been practiced primarily for self-protection and attacking and killing enemies. Movement of all types of martial arts clearly reflects these characteristics, and they should be practiced with the concept of combat in mind (Xi, 1984: 10, 26). Therefore, the practitioner of martial arts aims at pursuing fast, crisp, neat, powerful, and even violent movement, so that the goal of defense and attack can be achieved (Xi, et al., 1980: 2).

In Peking Opera, a large part of fighting movements are borrowed from the martial arts and are adapted for the stage (Pan, 1995: 23, 66). That is why many basic movement patterns of martial-acrobatic arts bear a strong resemblance to those of martial arts (Yao, 1990b: 179-183). However, the purpose of practicing martial arts changes when they are borrowed and applied to the theatrical arts. The effect of attacking and killing enemies is no longer important, but the display of movement becomes the major aim. Therefore, though stage combat and the martial forms look very similar, they are not exactly the same. In fact, Peking Opera adopts the external form of martial arts. Zhou Jiaxiang points out that Chinese theater adopts only the beautiful movement and gorgeous external appearance of Long Boxing (*Changquan*, the northern schools of martial arts), and almost discards completely real techniques of killing enemies. The aspect of fighting is sometimes displayed in a more abstract form, and occasionally it is exaggerated for the purpose of creating gallant images of heroes (Zhou, 1985: 65). Because martial arts are purposefully modified for the stage, they have lost their original violence and cruelty in the theater.

On the stage, martial-acrobatic arts merge with dance (Xu, 1991: 136-137). Each martial-acrobatic movement, whether performed in civil or fighting plays, is dance-like, and pleasant to the eye. The performance of martial-acrobatic arts in Peking Opera demonstrates form, rhythm, and balance, which are clearly dance elements.

The idea that fighting movements have to be aesthetically beautiful is greatly emphasized in Peking Opera. It is essential that the actor's postures are graceful while manipulating weapons (Cheng, 1981: 38). Particularly in the scenes of armed combat among generals, the movements of weapon manipulation must be elegant and visually pleasing, and can be viewed as refined dance movements (Qi, 1979: 3432, 3436). The unarmed movements also need to be beautiful. The martial-acrobatic arts' jumps, flips, turns, and kicks are not as powerful, violent, and masculine as they often are in martial forms; on the contrary, the emphasis is on the movements' line, shape, speed, skillfulness, and neatness (Wang, P., 1982: 1, 11, 81-82). Through these movements, a good performer, such as famous fighting actor Li Shaochun, is able to provide his audience powerful images of beauty (Weng, 1981: 47).

In Peking Opera, there are several special elements that help to change combat forms into dance forms. One of these is the stylized pose (*liangxiang*). It usually appears after a fighting scene or a sequence of martial-acrobatic movements. It is not realistic for a fighter to stop in the middle of a fight and make a stylized pose; therefore, the poses intermittently remind the audience that it is actually a dance rather than a real fight. They also provide the audience opportunities to applaud.

Another characteristic element is a single character's demonstration of the martial-acrobatic arts. Usually it is a solo performance by a major role, and he must very skillfully perform certain difficult stunts or weapon manipulation patterns. There are several different types of solo performance. One of these is *shua xiachang* (weapon manipulation before an exit), which is often seen in fighting scenes. After a fight, the winner stays on the stage and manipulates his weapon (or weapons) to show complacency (Qi, 1979: 3434). Oftentimes it is a chance for the actor to demonstrate his superb martial-acrobatic techniques and to win applause. A weapon routine before an exit is always visually beautiful and never fails to attract the audience. It demonstrates elegant and skillful movements and can certainly be viewed as an exquisite solo dance piece with props.

Music accompaniment is probably the most important element that makes martial-acrobatic movement closer to dance. In Peking Opera, all fighting scenes are accompanied by percussion music. Qi Rushan wrote:[3]

> We assume ideally that martial-acrobatic arts, when first used in drama, were not much different from real martial arts. More changes were made as more shows were performed, and gradually percussion music was added. Finally, the present form of martial-acrobatic arts was shaped. Therefore, though taken from martial arts, martial-acrobatic arts differ drastically from them. It can be said that martial arts are beautified.
> – Qi, 1979: 3436

In fact, martial-acrobatic arts are rhythmically regularized. There are many percussive patterns used in the combat scenes, and the actor's martial-acrobatic movements must intimately coordinate with those patterns (Yao, 1990c: 64-69). While fighting, he must listen carefully to the percussive music and sometimes provide signals to the drummer, who leads the orchestra, so that his movements and the music can be perfectly coordinated (Dai, 1990: 101-02, 117). A good fighting actor, such as Yang Xiaolou, is said to be able to coordinate beautifully with the percussive music while fighting with weapons (Dai, 1990: 112-113).

The actor cannot perform fighting movements without thinking of rhythm, tempo, and speed. The wugong's natural rhythm and tempo are somehow changed to suit the particular rhythm of the percussive music. For example, the music for the stylized pose makes obvious changes in the martial-acrobatic movement. Often, the pose, which immediately follows a series of martial-acrobatic movements, is accompanied by a heavy striking of the major percussive instruments, such as the drum and gongs. For the punctuation of the percussive instruments to synchronize with the pose, signals need to be provided to the drummer. Usually the method is to slightly slow down the several martial-acrobatic movements prior to the pose and to regularize their rhythm, making it easier for the drummer to catch the right moment for the striking of instruments. With the accompaniment of the percussive music, the martial-acrobatic forms are thus transformed into beautiful dance forms.

A Method of Creating a Role

In his later years, Konstantin Stanislavsky began to focus his attention on experiments of the actor's physical actions. His famous "Method of Physical Action" assists the actor in developing and enriching his body language. At that time, he regarded physical actions as the most important element of stage expressiveness, and he always demanded clearness and dexterity in their use by his actors (Toporkov, 1979: 163). Stanislavsky believed that an actor's appropriate and expressive bodily gestures were an effective means of creating a role. Vasily Toporkov, who had intimately worked with Stanislavsky, said:

> In his work as theatre director and teacher, Stanislavsky paid special attention to an actor's physical behavior in the process of creating a role. Stanislavsky knew that only a well-structured line of physical actions would enable the actor to create the precise outlines of the role.... – Toporkov, 1970: 524

Through the use of proper and logical physical actions, a role's characterization and emotion can be clearly revealed.

> Stanislavsky defined the actor as a "master of physical actions." Nothing so clearly, so convincingly transmits the spiritual condition of a person as his physical behavior; that is, as his sequence of physical actions. Not without reason do the most prominent masters of the stage make use of this knowledge....
> – Toporkov, 1979: 162

It is amazing to see certain similarities between the use of martial-acrobatic arts in Peking Opera and Stanislavsky's Physical Action Method. In Peking Opera, the martial-acrobatic arts are used to create roles. It is true that sometimes these arts may be performed to add spectacular effects, but they are not used for the sake of creating excitement only. If we take a closer look at the martial-acrobatic movements in many fighting plays created by earlier master actors, we will discover that most of the martial-acrobatic movements used in the performance bear certain meanings. In fact, combat is not performed to merely demonstrate skills; on the contrary, it is intimately integrated with acting. A fight should always show the spirit, character, and special circumstances of the combatants (Pan, 1995: 65). In the performance, the martial-acrobatic arts enlarge the character's expressive bodily vocabulary, adding more dimension to the movement, so that he can be much more physical. In addition, they are also used to display the role's characterization and emotion.

To explain how martial-acrobatic arts are used to create roles, a scene from *The Three-Forked Crossroad* is selected for analysis. The description of actors' movements is based on a film of a live performance, *Night at the Peking Opera*.[4] The film is widely available in the United States, and the scene is a popular one, which is why this scene is chosen.

This scene's plot is fairly simple.[5] Ren Tanghui, a gallant general who disguises himself as an ordinary warrior, goes into an inn intending to stay overnight. Liu Lihua, a cunning innkeeper, mistakes Ren for an enemy and wants to murder him. With a sword, Liu sneaks into the room where the general lodges, and they fight violently with each other in pitch darkness until a table leg hits Liu's left foot.

The martial-acrobatic arts performed in this scene from *The Three-Forked Crossroad* may generally be divided into two categories according to the nature of the movement: the more realistic and the abstract types. The first type refers to many basic patterns of the armed combat. They are self-explanatory, being somewhat stylized movements of armed combat.

The abstract type includes all the acrobatic movements, most of the unarmed martial movements, and a number of basic patterns of the armed combat. These movements are non-realistic and are actually symbols signifying various things. For example, acrobatic movement patterns such as somersaults or cartwheels are seen often in both fighting and non-fighting scenes. They may be used to symbolize flying in the air, climbing mountains, crossing rivers, jumping over walls, falling from horseback, etc. (Pan, 1987: 254). However, each stunt does not have specific, fixed meanings; on the contrary, its meanings vary, depending entirely on the given situation or circumstance of the scene. For instance, a somersault performed in one scene may represent the character flying in the air; the same somersault in another scene may indicate the character jumping over a wall. Because their meanings are changeable, the martial-acrobatic movements can be used very flexibly for creating roles. Stunts may be added to a scene if the actor feels it is necessary (Dai, 1990: 116-117); they may also be modified or replaced with other stunts as long as the change is appropriate to that particular situation (Beijing Zhengxie, 1990: 503-04).

After careful examination of all the martial-acrobatic movements in this scene, we discover that nearly all the movements of the abstract type have meaning. The following is a list of the major movement patterns performed in the scene, listed in order of appearance:

(1)	Crouched walk	*aibu*
(2)	Forward roll #1	*qianmao*
(3)	Aerial cartwheel from the table	*taiman*
(4)	Forward roll #2	*qianmao*
(5)	Backward roll #1	*daomao*
(6)	Circling leg kick over the head	*piantou*
(7)	Puhu[6] on the table	*shanggao puhu*
(8)	Iron-threshold	*tiemenkan*
(9)	Backward roll #2	*daomao*

The above seven patterns are used for distinct purposes in the scene. Their functions may be classified into three categories: movement stylization, emotion expression, and characterization development. Movement stylization is the simplest type of all functions and is readily understood. Oftentimes martial-acrobatic movements are taken to stylize certain realistic or life-like movements to make them more interesting or exciting. A good example is the *taiman* (aerial cartwheel from the table) performed by Ren. At the beginning of the scene, Liu and Ren suddenly find each other in the dark. At this point, Ren is on the table. He needs to get down and quickly begin a fight with his enemy. Instead of jumping or climbing down from the table, which is realistic and dull, Ren performs an aerial cartwheel from the table. Thus his movement is not only stylized, but also appears clean and neat.

A second example is found in the middle of the scene when Liu is bare-handed and Ren attacks him with a sword. At this moment, Liu performs a forward roll (forward roll #2) and a backward roll (backward roll #1). Since Liu is unarmed, he must try his best to avoid the assault. He bends down several times to elude Ren's violent attack, and then he performs the forward and backward rolls. These two stunts add variety to Liu's movements and make his simple movement of evasion much more lively and interesting.

The martial-acrobatic arts are also used to express the character's emotions. An example is found at the very beginning of the scene when Liu secretly enters with a sword. He walks in using *aibu*, the crouched walk, and suddenly performs a forward roll (forward roll #1). Because he is going to murder Ren, he walks stealthily, feeling very nervous (Guo, 1981: 23). This forward roll signifies that Liu accidentally stumbles during his stealthy approach because of extreme nervousness; in other words, his nervous feeling is conveyed externally through the movement of falling.

A second example is found at the very end of the scene. Ren suddenly throws down the table and Liu is struck heavily on the left foot by one of the table legs. At this moment, Liu begins to repeatedly perform a very difficult stunt called the *tiemenkan*. He lifts his left leg with bended knee and grasps his wounded left foot with his right hand, thus his left leg and right arm approximately form a semi-circle in front of the body. Then he jumps up, and in mid-air he extends his right leg outside the semi-circle and lands on the right leg. As soon as he lands on the floor, he jumps up again and draws his right leg back to the inside of the semi-circle. This stunt is repeated nine times. However, the performance of the tiemenkan is not a mere display of acrobatics, but an exaggeration of the excessive pain Liu feels. The continuous repetition of this stunt indicates the degree of pain. To exaggerate this pain even more, Liu performs a backward roll (backward roll #2) to symbolize the extreme suffering, which makes him roll on the floor.

To convey the characterization of a role is perhaps the most important function of the martial-acrobatic arts. In this scene, the two characters are quite different. Liu is a cunning owner of an inn where customers are murdered at night; whereas Ren is a general who is very gallant and upright. The drastic contrast of their personalities is expressed externally through specially selected martial-acrobatic movements. It is believed that stunts that involve contractive or huddling movements are more appropriate for villains because they suggest crookedness and surreptitiousness. At the very beginning of the scene, Liu enters the stage using the crouched walk. This movement pattern requires the lower part of his body to remain contracted. A second example is found in the middle of the scene when Liu is barehanded. As mentioned above, he performs both a forward and a backward roll to avoid Ren's attack. These two stunts again require his body to curl up. Thus Liu's slyness and lowliness are clearly expressed through carefully selected martial-acrobatic movements.

Ren's wugong movements differ from Liu's. In this scene, Ren never performs any stunt that involves rolling on the floor. Compared to Liu's contractive movements, Ren's movements are very open, extended, clear, and powerful, which reflect Ren's gallant and upright nature as well as his high rank. For example, at the beginning of the scene just before he starts to fight with Liu, Ren performs a taiman to get down. While executing this stunt, Ren throws his body in the air, lets it travel in a beautiful curve, and then lands in front of Liu. Though he is barehanded, he nevertheless prepares to fight. This sequence depicts Ren's brave and powerful qualities.

In the middle of the scene just after Liu kicks away Ren's sword, Ren executes a *piantou* (circling leg kick over the head) to attack Liu. This movement requires the performer to kick one of his legs up and draw a circle in the air, which again demonstrates an open, extended movement.

A third example is found shortly after the piantou is executed. As Liu jumps over the table and lands on the stage, Ren quickly leaps over the table, performing a *shanggao puhu* (*puhu* on the table). At the same time, he sweeps his legs toward Liu's head to assault him. As he executes this stunt, he leaps up and lands on the table with both hands. Being suspended in the air with feet raised higher than the waist, his body forms a nice curve. The movement of Ren swinging his open, curved body in the air toward Liu's head projects tremendous power and strength. Therefore, it is evident that Ren's martial-acrobatic movements are selected and arranged to signify his brave, candid, and superior qualities.

1) Aerial cartwheel (*taiman*). 2) Backward roll (*daomao*). 3) Crouched walk (*aibu*). 4) Circling kick over the head (*piantou*). 5) Jumping through the leg/arm semi-circle (*tiemenkan*). 6) Jumping through the leg/arm semi-circle (*tiemenkan*). *Illustrations by Huang Yuanting.*

The martial-acrobatic arts indeed play a significant role in Peking Opera. Actors of both fighting and non-fighting roles practice these arts to improve their health, strengthen their will power, and develop their physical abilities. They are used in both fighting and non-fighting plays to create dances or dance-actions and to help actors build their roles. In other words, the martial-acrobatic arts are absolutely essential to actors as well as the productions themselves. Without this precious element, the performance of Peking Opera will be much less physical, consequently losing its richness and attractiveness.'

APPENDIX
An Abbreviated Description of Movements in *The Three-Forked Crossroad*

The stage is empty with only a single table placed at the upstage center. Ren Tanghui is alone; he extinguishes the candle and lies on the table. Liu Lihua secretly enters with a sword from upstage right. He walks in a crouched walk (*aibu*). As he reaches stage right, he performs a forward roll (*qianmao*), and then immediately jumps up high with his body remaining crouched. He lands on the floor and crosses downstage in aibu. He mimes the movements of touching the door and opening it quietly. He stealthily crosses to the table in aibu and stands up. He fumbles in the dark, accidentally touching Ren's sword, which is underneath the latter's body. Liu quietly pulls out the sword.

At this moment, Ren wakes up and gets down from the table. The two men fumble in the dark. When Ren's hand accidentally touches Liu's hand, they are both startled. Liu promptly makes two strikes; at the same time Ren hastily jumps on the table. Trying to discover where his enemy is, Liu sits on the table and listens intently. They continue to fumble in the dark. Suddenly, they feel each other's breath, which stuns them. Ren slaps Liu on the face and performs an aerial cartwheel (*taiman*) from the table to get down.

They begin to fight with each other in the dark. Liu wildly attacks his enemy with two swords. Since Ren is unarmed, he tries his best to evade the attack. Then, both jumping up, Ren tightly grabs Liu's wrists. Thus together they strike a stylized pose (*liangxiang*).

After the pose, Ren continues to hold Liu's wrists. At the same time, the latter tries hard to shake off Ren's hands. Suddenly, Ren snatches a sword from Liu, and they hastily break away. They continue to fight violently with each other.

A moment later, Ren hits Liu's sword, which then springs directly toward the left wing. At this moment, Ren begins to attack Liu, taking nine quick sweeps with his sword. Since Liu is barehanded, it is his turn to try to evade his enemy's assault. Liu jumps up or dodges by bending over to avoid the attack. Then he performs a forward roll (*qianmao*) and a backward roll (*daomao*) to elude the sword. After he completes the backward roll, Liu hastily stands up and kicks Ren's sword with his right leg. As a result, Ren's sword flies toward the left wing.

The two men continue to fight empty handed. Ren does a circling leg kick over the head (*piantou*), and Liu bends to evade it. Ren then gives his enemy several heavy blows; as a result, Liu falls on the ground and rolls near the table. As Liu stands up, he promptly jumps over the table, and lands on the ground at the stage left side of the table.

Ren quickly runs toward the table and also jumps over it, performing a *puhu* on the table (*shanggao puhu*). As he jumps up, he sweeps his legs directly toward Liu's head, and then lands on the floor at the upstage side of the table. At the same time, Liu tilts his head to the right to avoid the attack. To chase each other, they move around the table. Coincidentally, each of them lifts the table from one end. They take three big steps sideways toward upstage while lifting the table together.

At this moment, Ren suddenly throws down the table. Being completely unprepared, Liu is struck heavily on the left foot by one of the table legs. He limps painfully, crossing downstage center. He grabs his wounded left foot and hops with one leg, making seven complete turns. Still hurt, he performs nine tiemenkan. Finally, he collapses on the floor, and then immediately performs a backward roll. After he completes the roll, he sits on the floor, rubbing his injured foot.

Acknowledgment

Special thanks to Cao Junlin, Huang Yuanting, Lee Minghsun, Li Pingping, Peng Cuihua, Wu Degui, and Zhu Luhao, for their kindness and assistance.

Notes

[1] Several months after this paper was completed, the school was renamed National Taiwan Junior College of Traditional Performing Arts.
[2] The "*qingyi*" is a role type which refers to virtuous young women. This roletype demands great singing techniques.
[3] Translated by the author.
[4] In the film, Zhang Yunxi plays Ren Tanghui, and Zhang Chunhua plays Liu

Lihua. Both actors are from China. The performance was filmed during a tour abroad in the early 1950's.

[5] Please see appendix for the plot of this scene and the description of movements. The appendix provides a general understanding of the plot line and where the martial-acrobatic movements discussed in this article are used. For a complete and detailed description of the actor's movements, see Yao, 1990c: 49-52.

[6] "*Puhu*" is difficult to translate. It is a sequence of movements in which a person jumps up and lands on the floor; as he lands on the floor, he uses his arms to support his body and lies face downwards. If a person jumps up and lands on a table, it is called "puhu on the table".

Bibliography

Beijing Zhengxie Wenshi Ziliao Yanjiu Weiyuanhui (Eds.). (1990). *Jingju tanwanglu sanpian* [Essays on the reminiscences of the Peking operas of the past, vol. 3]. Beijing: Beijing Chubanshe.

Chang, X. (1981, February). Yange yaoqiu ziji [To demand rigid discipline from oneself]. *Renmin Xiju*, 57-58.

Chang, X. (1981, May). Yanyuan yao ai sangzi, baohu jiashang duanlian [An actor must protect his vocal chords and develop his voice]. *Renmin Xiju*, 52-53.

Cheng, Y. (1981). *Cheng Yanqiu wenji* [Collected writings of Cheng Yanqiu]. Beijing: Zhongguo Xiju Chubanshe.

Dai, S., et al. (Eds.). (1990). *Yang Xiaolou yishu pinglun ji* [Critical essays on the art of Yang Xiaolou]. Beijing: Zhongguo Xiju Chubanshe.

Delza, S. (1972). T'ai-chi ch'uan: The integrated exercise. *The Drama Review* 16(1), 28-33.

Guan, S. (1979, April). Liangong han xueyi [Practicing the fundamental techniques and learning the art (of Peking opera)], *Renmin Xiju*, 40-42.

Guo, Y. (1981, December). Fei zhi wuyi chengxue—ji jingju ming wuchou Zhang Chunhua [Without perseverance there is no success—On the famous Peking opera fighting clown, Zhang Chunhua]. *Renmin xiju*, 20-23.

Hebeisheng Wenshi Ziliao Weiyuanhui (Eds.). (1986). *Wusheng taidou Gai Jiaotian* [The master fighting actor Gai Jiaotian]. Hebei: Hebei Renmin Chubanshe.

Liu, S. (1980). *Guoju jiaose han renwu* [Characters and actors of Peking opera]. Taipei: Liming Wenhua.

Mackerras, C. (Ed.). (1983). *Chinese theater: From its origins to the present day*. Honolulu: University of Hawaii Press.

Mei, L., & Xu, J. (Eds.). (1957). *Wutai shenghuo sishi nian* [Forty years of life on the stage], vol. 1. Beijing: Renmin Wenxue Chubanshe.

Nichols, R. (1991). "Way" for actors: Asian martial arts. *Theatre Topics* 1(1), 43-57.

Pan, X. (1987). *Jingju yishu wenda* [Questions and answers on the art of Peking opera]. Beijing: Wenhua Yishu Chubanshe.

Pan, X. (1995). *The stagecraft of Peking opera*. Beijing: New World Press.

Qi, R. (1979). *Qi Rushan quanji* [Complete works of Qi Rushan], vol. 6. Taipei: Lianjing Chubanshe.

Radium Film, Inc. (c. 1952). *Night at the Peking opera*. Chicago, IL: Radium Film, Inc.

Sun, X. (1980). *Xiqu wugong jiaocheng* [Methods of teaching the martial-acrobatic arts of Chinese opera]. Beijing: Zhongguo Xiju Chubanshe.

Toporkov, V. (1970). Physical actions. In T. Cole & H. Krich Chinoy (Eds.), *Actors on acting*. New York: Crown Publishers.

Toporkov, V., & Edwards, C. (Trans.). (1979). *Stanislavski in rehearsal*. New York: Theatre Arts Books.

Wang, J. (1983, June). Yu qingnian yanyuan tantan lian jibengong [A talk with young actors on the practice of the fundamental techniques of the martial-acrobatic arts]. *Xiju Bao*, 62-64.

Wang, P., et al. (1982). *Xiqu biaoyan tanzigong jiaocai* [Teaching materials for acrobatic techniques of Chinese opera]. Beijing: Zhongguo Xiju Chubanshe.

Weng, O. (1981, May). Li Shaochun biaoyan yishu de chenggong zhi lu [The road to the success of Li Shaochun's art]. *Renmin Xiju*, 42-48.

Xi, Y., et al. (1980). *Wushu de gongfang jishu* [Martial arts techniques of defense and attack]. Hong Kong: Shangwu Yinshuguan.

Xi, Y., et al. (1984). *Wushu jibengong* [Fundamental techniques of martial arts]. Hong Kong: Shangwu Yinshukuan.

Xu, C. (1991). *Mei Lanfang yu zhongguo wenhua* [Mei Lanfang and Chinese culture]. Taipei: Shangding Wenhua Chubanshe.

Yao, H. (1990a). The use of martial-acrobatic arts in the training and performance of Peking opera. Ph.D. diss., University of Minnesota.

Yao, H. (1990b). The influence of martial arts on the acting of traditional Chinese theater. *Yishu Pinglun* 2, 167-188.

Yao, H. (1990c). The relationship between percussive music and the movement of actors in Peking opera. *Journal of the Society for Asian Music* 21(2), 39-70.

Zhou, J. (1985, October). Beipai wushu jingshen zhi biaoshuai changquan [Long-boxing: A paragon of the spirit of the northern schools]. *Zhonghua guoshu*, 64-67.

Zhu, L. (1990, May 1). Personal interview with author in Taiwan.

· 3 ·

War and Worship:
Evolution of Martial Music and Dance in India

by Badana Mukhopadhyay, Ph.D.

A typical martial movement use in the Kathakali school of dance of Kerala State. *All photographs courtesy of Sangeet Natak Academy, New Delhi, India.*

The Historical Backdrop

The Indian subcontinent has a hoary tradition of assimilating people of various ethnic compositions. The reason is not difficult to understand. Over the centuries, stories of India's enormous wealth have lured invaders from all parts of the world to this subcontinent. As Basham observed:

> The ancient civilization of India grew up in a sharply demarcated sub-continent bounded on the north by the world's largest mountain range—the chain of the Himalayas, which, with its extensions to east and west divide India from the rest of Asia and the world. The barrier, however, was at no time an insuperable one, and at all periods both settlers and traders have found their way over the high and desolate passes into India, while Indians have carried their commerce and culture beyond her frontiers by the same route.
>
> – Basham, 1954: 1

Both archaeological and anthropological evidences validate the Indian oral tradition of myths and legends of bitter wars and the gradual merger of the marauding intruders with the older indigenous population in the subcontinent.

The earliest of the oral traditions is the *Rg Veda* where many hymns can be found referring to battles between one tribe and another, the underlying intertribal rivalry and a sense of solidarity with the indigenous groups who evidently represent the survivors. The importance accorded to music for battle and battlefields in the later epics like *Ramayana* and *Mahabharata* and the elaborate rituals associated with worship of martial musical instruments in the ancient Indian texts indicate that a culture of art and music was integrated with war since the very beginning. Today the martial arts survive, primarily among the indigenous people, the tribal communities, where martial dance and music are both acts of ritual to appease nature as well as entertainment for the community.

The earliest reference to a musical instrument exclusive to martial arts is perhaps the Vedic description of *dundhubi*, used by warring enemies in ancient times (Shakuntala, 1968). The dundhubi is a war drum whose sound is believed to charge up the warrior with vigor. Both the *Rig* and *Atharva Vedas* refer to this instrument and there are long pieces glorifying the powers of the battle drum. The dundhubi was a special sort of earth drum covered by hide of sacrificial animals like buffalo and even cow and is perhaps the largest of the percussion instruments described in the ancient texts. Such drums continued to be used by kings in the historical past and can be seen in museums of royal houses especially in Rajasthan, where the tradition of war is romanticized and life lost in battlefield is still the most coveted form of death. Apparently the war drum was a very precious possession of the warring groups because its capture meant defeat. This tradition of deciding the outcome of a duel by the capture of the war drum is popular sport among some of the tribal communities in India who are otherwise totally unrelated both culturally and demographically.

With time, a steady growth in the number of musical instruments used in martial activities and during war can be seen. There are references in the *Mahabharata* of armies marching to a battlefield to the rhythms of drums known as *bheri*, *shankha* and *mridanga*. Interestingly, over the centuries, across the subcontinent, these instruments have become associated with rituals which signify the beginning of a new phase.

The *nagara*, also known as a *bheri*, is a sort of big conical drum covered with hide. The diameter of its head is between two to three feet. A nagara was known to be used by royal families as the musical instrument heralding dawn or any auspicious event, like the birth of the male heir. Nagaras are a common sight in temples and one usually heads the ceremonial processions of deities during religious festivals.

The *shankha* (conch shell) is the musical instrument whose auspicious sound is still the most prevalent way to start religious functions among the Hindus. A hole is drilled at the base of the shell and as wind passes through the different whorls it produces a loud, sharp and piercing sound. In the *Mahabharata*, every important general carried his own shankha to the battleground and announced his intention to attack by blowing it.

The *mridanga*, made out of burnt clay closely covered with strips of leather lacing, can produce a deep bass sound. It has come to be associated with the classical musical form known as *dhrupad*. Smaller sized mridangas, known as *khol*, are played as a popular accompaniment to choral devotional songs called *kirtans* among *Vaishnavites* (followers of a Krishna cult, popular in Bengal, Tripura, Manipur).

Jataka stories from the Buddhist tradition, written a few centuries after the birth of Buddha, describe more elaborate sets of musical instruments associated with war and martial activities. The *Sonandha Jataka* refers to a variety of musical instruments designed and grouped in a way that gave a harmonious effect to the sounds created. While the tradition of the conch shell and dundhubhi to herald the return of a victorious king [has] remained unchanged with the passage of time, the Jataka references present a few more familiar musical instruments like the *dhak,* a lotus-shape mouthed drum, very large in size and with a robust sound that reverberates reaching out far and wide (Shakuntala, 1968). A somewhat smaller size drum, still known as the dhak, continues to be an integral part of the Dassera festivals in Bengal where the tradition is of the worship of a female deity, the Durga, after her triumphant return from a daring war with a demon, dreaded even by the gods. In fact a study of the ancient Indian mythologies show there is a very close connection between war and worship in the Indian way of life.

The Folk Tradition of Martial Music

To understand the martial music of the subcontinent, it is important to study the martial traditions in folk and tribal cultures in the country. Interestingly, the Punjab (which is believed to have faced the largest number of invading tribes coming from west and northwest) has only a musical tradition of martial arts, while in the northeast (where there is less historical evidence of invasion and even fewer legends of conquest by armies beyond the geographical boundaries) the martial traditions combine invigorating dance forms, music and ritualistic ceremonies. Anthropologists believe that the martial traditions among the tribes in northeastern India have developed as a result of continuous inter-tribal rivalry which necessitated constant preparedness on the part of the able bodied men. Martial dances and songs served both as entertainment and for the constant sharpening of skills (Folk Culture of Manipur, n.d.: 45-46).

The most popular martial music from Punjab is the *Vaar Geet*. These are ballads, and the vaar poetry forms a significant part of the oral tradition in Punjab's folk literature. Vaar is usually sung by two groups of men, who are both narrators and protagonists. Dressed in their traditional colorful attire, complete with turban and the now famous Punjab-style jacket, with a range of martial implements like the sword, shield, spear, etc, they sit on the stage and sing without any musical accompaniment, except a small drum, and with stylized movements, pick up different martial instruments, adding a visual impact to the unfolding of the tale they are narrating. Mostly the poetry is about heroic kings who were heroes in every field, and a hero because he would never run away from a battlefield. Romanticized tales about the tenth Sikh Guru, Govind Singh, who added a martial tradition in the Sikh religion, is understandably a popular subject of Vaar Geet.

The drum plays a very important part in the folk music of Punjab. It provides the basic accompaniment to most of folk music. The *dhol* and *dholik* (also known as *dholki*), the male and female drums, had their own relevant use. These drum beats once signalled the approached of an impending army and information used to be quickly passed around to the neighboring villages through a particular beat.

Vaar Geet performance.

Another form of Vaar, known as *Kavishree,* deals with mythical heroes, kings and war of the gods. The poetry of Kavishree is more narrative and the presentation more colorful. These songs also provide an insight into the importance accorded to supernatural powers in perfecting martial techniques. Three or four singers form two groups and sing with stylized physical movements using martial implements such as the sword, shield, dagger and the like. These physical movements are comparatively recent additions created in response to the demands for a more colorful stage presentation (Dhillon, 1998: 89-90).

An interesting martial musical tradition in the Punjab is found among the wrestlers living in every village. While they practiced at their traditional school (*akhara*), a very typical music grew around their practice and has come to be known as "akhara singing." The instruments used in akhara music are typically common to any household and largely drawn from the kitchen or made by the performers in their leisure time. All of these percussion instruments are made of different kinds of basic materials, like wood, metal, and animal hide. According to Vaar singer Moola Singh Dhadhi (personal communication, June 1999), many of them have become very popular accompaniments to different kinds of traditional music of the Punjab.

Among the martial dances, some can be easily identified as a martial form, but many are so stylized that only a careful analysis reveals their martial character. One example is the *Chholia* dance, which is popular in the sub-Himalayan Kumaon region. Traditionally, this dance used to be performed only by men with swords and shields and utilizing steps to depict mock combat of attack and defense. The musical accompaniment was also typically martial: a "U"-shaped trumpet, a horn, and a few drums to pick up the rhythmic beats. But over the years this dance has come to be linked to a strange festival associated with a local flower known as *kirji*. The kirji is an extremely poisonous flower that blooms once in twelve years. When kirjis bloom, the villagers, both men and women, dance the Chholia in processions to destroy the new blooms so that its pollen or petals do not contaminate the water sources and make drinking water scarce (Pani, 2002: 96). These days Chholia is becoming a popular entertainment in wedding processions where the party accompanying the groom enjoy showing their might as they reach the bride's home. It is difficult to recognize the martial origin of the dance when it is performed on such occasions.

The three states along the western borders of the Republic of India—Punjab, Rajasthan and Gujarat—have very distinct martial arts traditions. The underlying sentiment in all their music, however, is an intense attachment to family honor, which transcends the honor of the motherland. The *Gair* of the Mewar region in western Rajasthan is a vigorous dance where inner and outer circles of dancers move diagonally or loop in and out. It is intricate and fascinating. The Gair of Jodhpur is performed in a single file and martial costumes are worn for effect.

Mehr Rass performance.

The *Geendad* of Shekhawati is similar to the Gair. Sticks or swords are often used in male dances, and the Shekhawati dance has the daft accompanying it. The musical accompaniment to these dances is merely to hold together the fast pace of the dance.

In most martial dances from Western India, sticks play a very significant role. Sticks act both as a combat weapon as well as an interesting part of the total costume where the stick becomes an integral part of the stylized movements for the dancers. The most well known among the dances using stick is the *Dandiya Raas* (stick dance) from the Kathiawar region of Gujarat. Performed by both men and women, Dandiya is perhaps the most colorful of the folk forms among Indian dances. It has been urbanized with an element of fun and frolic by appending parts of the legend of Krishna into the musical content, making the dance an integral part of the socio-religious festivals of Gujarat today (Shukla, n.d.). The original form of Dandiya, now found only in the Kuchh region, was purely martial. Known as *Mehr Raas*, this dance used to be performed only by men with sticks in their hands and drum-beats controlling the intricate rhythmic pattern of the movements. Mehr Raas is visually much less entertaining than the Kathiawar Dandiya which is fast becoming a subject for archivists of musical traditions (Dhillon, 1998).

Stick-fighting practice of Kalarippayaatu.

The story of Vadakkan Pattukkal, once a popular folk style in Kerala, is similar. A lucky tourist may chance upon bands of singers in the villages of North Malabar, singing heroic deeds of valiant soldiers, giving details of their attire, weapons, dress and martial techniques they had adopted to win the battle. These bands of singers, once a common enough sight throughout Kerala are today almost a vanishing tribe. Their music, known as *Vadakkan Pattakkal*, is mostly available in the sound archives of All India Radio and Sangeet Natak Academy.

Many of the Vadakkan Pattukkal or northern ballads of Kerala songs are about *Kalarippayattu*, the most ancient among the living traditions of martial arts in the subcontinent. Scholars of Kalarippayatu trace back its origin to the *Dhanurveda*, the ancient Indian treatise for warfare (Pani, 1956). Historical evidence too can date Kalarippayatu to the 9th century C.E. (Nair, 1966). The word *kalari* is the local term for schools of physical culture and martial training, similar to the akharas in Punjab and Gangetic valley, where martial training is taught through ritualistic and spiritual education. The most important aspect of Kalarippayatu is the training which is long and intense and is controlled by the teacher through a series of verbal commands known as *vaythari*.

Kerala is in fact rich in martial folk traditions. The Ambalppuzha region in the western coast developed the *Vedakali*, a martial performing tradition to recreate the war fought by the Dutch and the Portuguese with the local king. Such is the admiration for those who fought and repelled the western seafarers that this dance has found a place among the dances preformed within a temple courtyard! This is a group dance performed with percussion instruments to accompany the dancers' steps, and wind instruments to keep tune and control the rhythm. A part of the audience stands behind the dancers and vocalise meaningless syllables to energize the dancers.

Vedakali dancers.

But even the best performers of martial music and dance in these states have remained performers. They are never regarded as on a par with the heroes whose valor they sing nor do they have any special position within their communities. Such an attitude is in complete contrast to the status of martial arts performers in the eastern part of the subcontinent. In Orissa, where traditional martial art forms have evolved into classical styles, the folk artists of martial dance and music are hailed as local heroes, almost identifying the performer with the central character of the narrative (Banerji, 1982).

A very popular martial dance form from Orissa, *Ghumura* is a fine example of this attitude. Ghumura is a form of traditional war music and dance from the Kalahandi district of Orissa. The lead dancer of a ghumura group is not only a local hero but is very much a leader in the community. Ghumura research scholar, singer and lyricist, Satyanarayan Nayak from Gour Sargiguda, says "Ghumura artist may be a farmer or a laborer or even a businessman or service holder who practices ghumura in his leisure time. But when he performs, he is charged with the divine power of the gods he portrays and that makes him superhuman in the eyes of the people who come to watch him perform" (field recordings by the author, n.d.).

The name Ghumura comes from the musical instrument essential to the performance. A *ghumura* is a small earthen pot with a long neck; the belly of the pot is round and the back had a hole and a nipple. The face of the pot is covered with the skin of an iguana, pasted with catechu gum to the earthen body and tightened with a rope. The ghumura is tied to the neck of the dancer who plays the instrument with both hands while he dances and sings. The performance is usually by a group of 15 to 20 artists with one lead dancer and singer, traditionally all men, though in recent times women are known to have taken part in some urban performances. Musical accompaniments include a iron bowl covered by cattle skin (*nishan*), brazen cymbals, war trumpets, tinkling trinkets tied at the feet of the dancers and rhythmic clapping by dancers as well as the public. The performance invariably begins with the blowing of conch shells and with an invocation to Manikeswari, the local goddess of war. A typical ghumura song (field recordings by the author, n.d.) can be as follows:

> Let the ghumura beat like the thunder of Indra.
> The rain god marches with the soldiers of Kalahandi.
> The fiery and deep sound of the iron bowl excites the soldier.
> Its sound resonates and inspires soldiers to jump into the war with a roar.
> It's the music of the heroes and the brave.
> Chant unitedly "Victory to Manikeswari"!*

> *Field recordings by the author, n.d.

An interesting feature of Ghumura is the dress of the dancers. It is strangely reminiscent of the Rajput dress and headgear—the warrior community of Rajasthan living almost 2,000 miles away, with no apparent social similarities or physical contact with the people of Orissa. Another interesting aspect of ghumura is an occasional complete lack of any martial reference in the content of the song that accompanies the totally martial movements of the dance. For instance, another popular Ghumura song (field recordings by the author, n.d.) is:

> What a time, what terrible time it is now!
> The odorless butea frondosa has become
> The king where once rose was supreme.
> Crow is now the court bird.
> Where has the peacock vanished?
> The stinging nettle is crowned and honored
> While the basil plant gets uprooted.
> What an ugly time! What terrible time has come!*

In the recent years, Ghumura has come into great focus because it could be easily adapted to propagate social messages: the lead dancer and singer is respected in the community, its language and form are familiar to the audience who are also comfortable with the concept of a totally different sentiment expressed in the songs while the dance continues to be exciting with expected martial movements (Mahapatra, 1999).

It is believed that in ancient times, the reign of the king of Orissa extended from the southern banks of the Ganges River in the north, to the northern borders of the Godavari River in the south. Such a large kingdom needed constant vigilance and the king of Orissa encouraged the soldiers to develop stylized martial movements as entertainment for the soldiers while they moved from one part of the kingdom to another. The kingdom is long lost but among certain caste groups in Khurda, Nayagarh, and Puri regions, the tradition of a battlefield dance is still popular. This unconscious rehearsal of battle movements has led to what is now known as the Paika Dance, which is still performed to resemble soldiers moving in a pattern of swordplay and to the accompaniment of music created with local drums called *tikura* and *chenga,* a country variety of tambourine played with sticks. This dance is one of the most dangerous among the martial folk traditions in the subcontinent because the slightest mistake can cause serious injury (Pani, 202).

In all these regions, traditions of martial music form a popular segment of folk entertainment. But among the tribal communities living in the northeastern region, martial dance and music is no leisure time entertainment, but a significant aspect of their way of life. The most interesting range of martial movements known in the subcontinent is to be found among the Nagas, the Khasis, the Manipuris, and the tribal communities from Arunachal Pradesh, Meghalaya and Mizoram. Racially these communities are closer to the Mongoloid group. They live in the forests, valleys and hills of the sub-Himalayan region and speak in dialects close to the Austro-Asiatic and Tibeto-Burman language groups (Shankar, 1974). Many of these tribes had been head-hunters in the not too distant past and are comfortable with hunting and killing to settle scores or establish command. Many of their ceremonial dresses, especially among the Naga men, are decorated with skulls and other trophies of war and the grand finale of most of their social celebrations is with the sacrifice of a chosen animal while a war dance is performed by the community. Dr. Kapila Vatsayan in her description of a typical Sema Naga tribe writes:

> The use of spear is common. In a typical dance, the dancers first enter in a single file to chorus singing or in reality to a cluster of sounds. The steps are characterised by a hop. This is followed by a pause. The body is invariably held straight as one unit. The formations are beautiful for their precision and their synchronisation. The line then transforms itself into a single circle, as the tempo increases. In the next phase two concentric circles are formed. Each dancer brandishes spears over-head and seems to attack invisible enemies. Next, he rapidly thrusts at his own limbs while successfully seeming to escape the attack of his own weapons. The dance ends in a crescendo of shouts, cries and sounds.
> — Vatsayan, 1976: 75

Martial dance among the Naga tribes is more famous for its physical movements than its musical accompaniments. The martial dance of *Khasis* is richer in its musical content. Their sword dance (*Ka Shad Mastieh*) is arranged with the most enchanting music central to which is their war drum and an indigenous wind instrument called *Ka Tangmuri*. The dance is essentially a duel with swords to settle a dispute. It is now a regular feature in the local festivities but from the movements it is obvious that the dance has developed as a practice exercise for real sword fights. Two dancers spar with swords, trying to cut each other's earrings from their lobes or the necklace from their necks. The one who succeeds first is declared the winner and is rewarded. A typical Khasi song accompanied by the wind instrument is:

> The Khynriams. The Pnars. The Bhois and the Wars.
> Together they form a huge khasi community.
> They are the well-armed children of bows and arrows.
> Like small flowers who absorb heavenly dews,
> They grow steadily. Steadily they grow.
> They have to develop a personality and carry on our responsibility.
> Oh blessed land! Oh my blessed land!
> It is you who will bless the brave children of the motherland!
> — Translated by E.B.R. Wanswett *

* Translated for the author by E. Wanswett, a Khasi folk singer from Shillong, 20 Sept. 1999.

Many of the folk traditions refer to hard and bitter battles fought with bands of people who later settled in the subcontinent and merged with the indigenous peoples. These folklores also provide an insight into the importance accorded to perfecting martial techniques by the victor as well as the vanquished through the invocation of supernatural powers. In addition to the custom of showing off martial prowess to assure the community of their capacity to successfully defend themselves, gradually martial performance gave rise to socio-religious rituals which included stylized performances to please local deities or ward off evil powers. For instance, *Thang Ta*, the sword and spear dance of the Manipuris, is their art of self-defense. Traditionally there was no music associated with Thang Ta. As its entertainment component became more important and Thang Ta began be performed as a regular feature in their royal festivals like Kwak-Taanba or Khou-Chonba, Thang Ta also found identification with local rituals to drive away evil spirits or prevent natural calamities. Today Thang Ta is an integral part of the famous Manipuri festival Lai-Haroba and has a distinctive musical base.

Another martial dance, *Pathet-Haiba*, performed mainly by the Marings, a tribal community in Manipur, still retains its supernatural flavor and is usually performed only during special rituals. Tokeswari Elangbam, Program Executive for All India Radio, says the only accompaniment to these dances is the drumbeat, which is typical for each occasion so that by the very first stroke, the audience knows what is to be performed (personal communication, n.d.). Manipur folk ballads are full of songs in praise of the brave and heroic ancestors. A typical Manipuri ballad sung either to the beat of the drum or the fiddle is:

> Oh father Sorarel (Sky God)
> Be pleased to give me a match.
> Be pleased to provide me a rival.
> Life is for fighting,
> Fighting the wild elephant,
> and coat its teeth with yellow dust.
> – Folk Culture of Manipur, n.d.: 49

In Arunachal Pradesh, many of their martial dances center around animals. One very attractive dance is the cockfight dance, known popularly as the *Ka-kong Tong-kai*. It is performed by two groups and each group is led by the head drummer dressed in spotted breeches and skirts with a headgear that resembles cock heads. A party of boys common to both groups play gongs and cymbals. The dancers stand face-to-face and their movements resemble the forward backward confrontations of two sets of proud and hostile cocks.

In different parts of India these martial traditions generated different kinds of music and dance, but the similarity in their origin cannot be mistaken. In northeastern India, martial traditions have become ceremonial rituals, and

Left: Use of weapons in Thang Ta. **Middle:** Pathet-Haiba—dance of the Naga tribes of Manipur State. **Right:** Typical attire for the martial dance called Ka-kong Tong-kai which originates from Arunachal Pradesh State.

there are tribal groups even today who take the traditions so seriously that they refuse to perform for mere entertainment. In contrast, in the western states like Punjab, Gujarat, and Rajasthan, martial traditions have undergone a synthesis with popular entertainment through film and cultural shows. But the socio-musical structure of the songs, the strange kind of frenzy associated with their performances and audience participation make the martial origin of the forms obvious even to the uninitiated viewer.

Evolution of Stylized Martial Dance Forms

Eminent scholar of *Chhau* dance, Jiwan Pani (2002), in his book writes:

> Deep in the past, before guns thundered the age old weapons off stage, men-at-arms used to parade rhythmically their mastery over weighty weapons like the sword, shield, club, spear or bow. To keep up the mastery, they also held a sort of mock fight in which, to the beat of the huge war drums, one group used to attack the other or defend themselves in turn. This gave rise to a form of martial dance named *Rookmar* or *Pharikhand Khela*. The Chhau of today gradually took shape out of this basic war dance and grew to classical heights with elaborate stylisation and developed a grammar of its own.

Three different yet closely similar styles of Chhau dance, all developed from rich tribal cultures in the regions, are popular: Chhau of Saraikela in Bihar, Chhau of Mayurbhanj in Orissa and Chhau from Purulia in West Bengal. All these areas, geographically within a radius of not more than 100 miles, developed this style according to their taste, patronage and resources.

Chhau in all probability began as a performance for the appeasement of forest gods, rain gods, the annual worship of the sun god and similar rituals.

The word *chhau* has three colloquial derivations: 1) *chauni*, meaning military camp, 2) *chhauri*, meaning attack and 3) *chchauka*, meaning the quality of stealthily attacking the enemy. All these root words, however, have a single reference point: warfare. A likely origin of the word from aboriginal sources is also possible because the Mundari tribe, who made important contributions to the Purulia Chhau, still use the words *Chhak Susun* for their Dance of Ghosts. Scholars believe that Chhau was initially a dance of ghosts and goblins or the followers of Shiva, before the cult of the mother goddess and the legend of Durga (consort of Shiva and the slayer of the demon Mahisashura) became central to the performance of Chhau. In fact Chhau dance, with its elaborate masks (Mayurbhanj Chhau is uniquely different because it does not use the mask, an essential in the other two styles) and weapons is famous for its artistic grandeur using martial movements and stylized presentation of mythological stories of war, episodes from the *Ramayana* and the *Mahabharata*, and is perhaps the only truly folk form accepted within the classical repertoire of Indian dance (Bhattacharya, 1976).

Chhau martial dance of Orissa State.

The music of Chhau is elaborate. In Mayurbhanj, the musical instruments accompanying the dance are: *dhol* (a barrel-shaped drum played with the palm and fingers of the left hand and a short stick in the right hand), *tikara* or *nagara, dhumsa, mahori* and *dhadi ladi*. Every performance begins with a vocal invocation to the elephant-headed god, Ganesha, who according to Hindu mythology is the son of Shiva. As soon as the vocalist stops, drums begin to beat loudly and the actual performance starts. The vocal music is not very impressive but the intricate percussion accompanying the dance is unique and rarely matched even in many classical forms. Performances usually begin after dinner and continue all through the night. In recent years, some innovations have been introduced in the Chhau dances and occasionally even political issues are popularized through Chhau performances.

Perhaps the most spectacular of all the martial forms is the dance drama from Kerala, *Kathakali*. Here is a unique confluence of performance genres: classical, folk, ritual, as well as martial. The exact process by which all these forms were welded into a new form is today difficult to trace but the obvious closeness between the martial practices and spirit of Kalarippayattu and the technique and spirit of Kathakali is an indicator of the martial component in Kathakali (Zarrilli, 1984: 41-55).

Not much ethno-musical or even socio-musical study has been done on this genre of Indian music or dance and consequently, standardized information on martial traditions in Indian creative arts is difficult to find. But a recent successful experiment using ghumura to propagate the importance of preserving forests in the famine-struck Kalahandi region of the Orissa state in eastern India has added another dimension to martial music traditions and has helped to bring into focus the need to collect, preserve and study these art forms. While systematic study of martial arts in India by native scholars has yet to start in a big way,* taking a cue from the spontaneous response by the local communities to non-traditional subjects as the theme for a performance, projects are being taken up using traditional martial art forms to create campaigns on important social issues such as malaria eradication, care for female children, education and health, branding them as themes of war, thus creating public awareness through traditional communication skills. From the saga of the epics and mythological wars to war against corrupt practices and social evils, the martial music of India is a living example of how the tradition and the contemporary merge in the cultural fabric of modern India.

* EDITOR'S NOTE
In an e-mail to our office (17 April 2002), the author writes that this statement "is a comment on the paucity of scholarly research by Indians in this field. I believe it is the works of researchers like Mr. Zarrilli that have brought Kerala martial arts to the notice of the intellectual establishment in India and abroad." For further readings of academic merit, see:

- Alter, J. (1992). *The wrestler's body: Identity and ideology in North India.* University of California Press.www.ucpress.edu
- Sangeet Natak Academy. Rabindra Bhawan, New Delhi 110 001 India. www.sangeetnatak.com
- Zarrilli, P. Articles in the *Journal of Asian Martial Arts*: Volume 1 Number 1, 1992; Volume 4 Number 1, 1995.
- Zarrilli, P. (2000). *When the body becomes all eyes: Paradigms, discourses and practices of power in Kalarippayattu, a South Indian martial art.* Oxford University Press. www.oup-usa.org

Bibliography

Banerji, P. (1982). *Aesthetics of Indian folk dance.* Delhi: Cosmo Publication.

Basham, A. (1954). *The wonder that was India.* New York: Grove Press.

Bhattacharya, A. (1976). *Chhau dance of Purulia.* Calcutta: Rabindra Bharati University Publication.

Dhillon, I. (1998). *Folk dances of Punjab.* Delhi: National Book Shop.

Folk Culture of Manipur. (n.d.). Imphal: Manipur State Publications.

Mahapatra, S. (1999, February 9). Interview. Bhawanipatna: All India Radio.

Nair, V. (1966, April). Innovations in Kathakali. *Sangeet Natak Academy Journal.*

Pani, J. (2002). *Indian folk dances.* New Delhi: Government of India, Publication Division.

Sarkar, N. (1974). *Dances of Arunachal Pradesh.* Shillong: Arunachal Pradesh Administration.

Shakuntala, K. (1968, December). Martial musical instruments of ancient India, *Sangeet Natak Academy Journal.*

Shukla, H. (n.d.). *Folk dances of Gujarat.* Ahmedabad: Government of Gujarat State, Central Press.

Vatsayan, K. (1976). *Traditions of Indian folk dance.* Indian Book Company.

Zarrilli, P. (1984). *The Kathakali complex: Actor, performance, structure.* New Delhi: Abhinav Publications.

· 4 ·

Ulla Werbrouck: Olympic and European Judo Champion Retires

by David Finch

All photos courtesy of Judo Photos Unlimited.

On the final day of the 2002 Wuppertal German World Open (23-24 February), 1996 Olympic champion Ulla Werbrouck of Belgium retired from competition judo. Her international career started in 1987 when she won a silver medal at the Junior German Open at Hamm and culminated in spectacular style with the 72 kgs (158.7 lbs.) Olympic title at Atlanta. She retires as the current 70 kgs (154 lbs.) European champion and since 1994 had accumulated seven European light heavyweight titles.

Ulla Werbrouck is not a stranger to North America: She reached seventh place in the Hamilton (Canada) 1993 World Championships, won the Atlanta Olympics 72 kgs (158.7 lbs.) gold medal, and won a gold medal at the 1998 US Open at Colorado Springs. She has even trained in Cuba, where her most serious opponents came from: Veranes, who beat her for the gold medal at the 1999 Birmingham World Championships, and Luna Castellano who took the 1995 World title from under her nose by a whisker. Over the past ten years, she has resoundly beaten her US competitors: Jiveden lost at the 1995 Tokyo

Worlds; D'Anya Bierria lost at the 1997 Paris Worlds and the 1999 Munich World Masters; and Sandra Bacher lost at the 1999 Munich World Masters and 2001 Munich Worlds. So, Werbrouck's retirement will come as a relief to United States judo.

It was not a coincidence that Werbrouck's announcement that she would retire from competition at the German World Open followed her dismal display at the Tourni de Paris two weeks earlier and a few days after her thirtieth birthday. There, Werbrouck—one of the few 'big hitters' in women's judo and a national heroine in Belgium with the car license plate of JUDO 43—had lost in the first round by a "small advantage" (*koka*) and then a throw that lacked the enough quality to score a full-point (*wazari*) in the *repercharge*.[1]

---

[1] The repercharge is a tournament judo system where the contestants beaten by the four semi-finalists in each weight category fight each other to fight the loser of the semi-final contests. This contest is then known as the "bronze medal contest" and there are two bronze medals in judo.

Coincidentally, the last time she had lost so badly was at the February 1998 Paris Tournament when she crashed out to a tremendous scoring point by an unrated rival and failed to make the repercharge. But the reasons then were very different. In her efforts to add the October 1997 world title to her Olympic crown, she had badly damaged her shoulder ligaments at a training camp in Cuba and could only manage a World bronze. It was the same nagging injury that started the 1998 season off so badly.

Ulla Werbrouck's next tournament was the Munich World Masters, two weeks later. There she reached the final, but for the first time in several meetings lost to 1996 Olympic bronze medalist Ylenia Scapin, an Italian fighter three years her junior. They met again in the final of the 1999 Wroclaw (Poland) Europeans, where Werbrouck returned to form and in an early flurry of action took both to the ground with Werbrouck in a dominant position on top. She systematically tied up Scapin with a "chest hold" (*mune-gatame*) and "cuddled the upstart" into submission. At the same time, Werbrouck set a European record as the first person to win six consecutive gold medals. Along with the rest of the Belgian team, she went wild and her longtime coach, Jean-Marie Dedecker, could not restrain his feelings, almost weeping with delight on her shoulder.

Werbrouck dominated further meetings with Scapin until they met in the third round of this year's Wuppertal German World Open. There, in front of over 400 yellow-shirted and "Werbrouck" chanting Belgian supporters, Scapin floored Werbrouck with a left major inner throw (*ouchi-gari*, see picture) for the only score of the match, a minor "small advantage." But the damage had been done and Werbrouck was prevented from retiring in style. She fought back through the repercharge with several spectacular throws and bowed out to her loyal and jubilant fans on the podium with a bronze medal.

All day, her mentor and coach, Jean-Marie Dedecker, had been at mat side, urging her on and sharing in the sadness of her farewell speech that afternoon. He had first spotted her as a 13-year-old Belgian junior champion in 1985. He quickly convinced her and her parents that she needed to train with the Belgian National Team. Four years later, she had won two European Junior 72 kgs (158.7 lbs.) titles and took the 66 kgs (145.5 lbs.) senior bronze medal at the Helsinki Europeans, where Belgian Ingrid Berghmans fought at the heavier weight. The following year, she won the Junior World 72 kgs gold medal, ideally placing her to take over the mantle of the Belgian heroine and world legend, Ingrid Berghmans, who was about to retire from competition.

There is nobody more responsible for the success of Ulla Werbrouck and Belgian judo than Jean-Marie Dedecker. Now an elected Belgian senator and astute businessman, he is consistently gaining the best sponsorship for Belgian judo; even now, he personally sponsors six judo fighters and athletes from other sports, including figure skating and the triathlon. But his first love is judo. In twenty years at the top, he has masterminded the winning of more than 130 Olympic, World, and European judo medals for one of the smaller countries of the world. His team even took six of the sixteen gold medals at the 1997 European Championships; an unprecedented feat.

At the 1996 Atlanta Olympics, Ulla Werbrouck reached the pinnacle of her career. This followed a particularly disappointing world silver medal the previous year at the Mukuhari (Japan) Worlds, when she lost on a referee's split decision. In fact, in six senior World Championships (earning her two silver and two bronze medals), this was the closest she ever came to winning the title that she craved, losing to Diadenis Luna Castellano of Cuba, whose hyperactive and persistent aggressiveness prevented Werbrouck from getting into position for a clean attack, relegating her to be considered the most passive of the two fighters. The defeat made her more determined and, luckily for Werbrouck, Luna Castellano was in the other pool at Atlanta, along with the two other front-runners for the title, Essombe of France and Tanabe Yoko of Japan. Tanabe emerged at the top of the other table following earlier point wins with her favorite left throw to the inner thigh. Werbrouck sailed through her half with a variety of holds and throws culminating with her favorite right uchimata throw for the winning point in the semi-final.

    The final was to be dominated by the inner thigh throws of both women. Tanabe was six years older than Werbrouck and nearly the same height of 5 feet 8 inches (1.79m). She already had an Olympic silver and bronze medal to her credit and was determined to improve on that. She attacked first, with her left inner thigh throw and was easily pushed aside by Werbrouck as the attack lacked penetration. Werbrouck followed up with a left counter sweep and scored a technical point.

Troubled by the score, Tanabe again attacked with a fiercer left inner thigh throw, taking Werbrouck scorelessly to the mat. Then, hovering close to the red area, Werbrouck unleashed her right inner thigh throw, almost head diving into the mat but rolling over her right arm and elbow to prevent a penalty and putting Tanabe heavily on her side and another technical point on the board. Trailing by two five-point scores (*yuko*) and with only a few seconds of the contest left, out of exasperation, Tanabe came in for her third and even fiercer left inner thigh throw. By this time, Werbrouck aware of the pattern, side-stepped the furious attack and easily slipped her right leg over Tanabe's flying left. In an almost body drop like position (see photo), and with only two seconds left on the clock, she pivoted Tanabe over her own hands heavily onto the mat. The result was a perfect inner thigh sweep (*uchimata sukashi*) for a full point and the Olympic title, followed by a deliriously ecstatic Werbrouck (see photo).

Ulla Werbrouck, who enjoys wearing high heels to increase her height and feminine charms after judo training, married Dimitri Himpe in January 1998 and at the time said, "I have no plans for children until after the 2000 Sydney Olympics." With the Olympics nearly two years ago, are children now on her mind or is it even possible that her first child is on the way?

· 5 ·

The Art of Conversation: Random Flow Training in Visayan Corto Kadena Eskrima

by Maija Soderholm, B.Sc.

VISAYAN CORTO KADENA ESKRIMA is the name Sonny Umpad has given to his martial art system. Visayan refers to the Visayan Islands of the central Philippines where Umpad grew up. Corto Kadena means "short chain," and has many levels of meaning from the physical to the philosophical. Eskrima has the same root as the word "skirmish," therefore it can be loosely translated as "fighting art."

Introduction

This article is about the art of Visayan Corto Kadena Eskrima and some of its concepts and training methods with regard to free-sparring with swords. It is a Filipino martial system encompassing empty-hand and non-bladed and bladed weapons. Its principles, however, are based on the sword. It is essentially a dueling art that, in times past, would leave only one participant standing.

Unlike empty-hand or even stick fighting, dueling with swords offers no forgiveness. A mistake in timing or reaction does not lead to a bruise or a broken arm, but to severed tendons, deep trauma, and potentially death. A much greater emphasis is therefore placed on strategy than perhaps would be with less lethal weapons.

As those who spar with weapons know, to hit a target is not too difficult, but to hit a target and "get out clean," without taking a hit, is much harder. However, this must be the goal. Thankfully, today we do not have to prove our skill in challenge matches with live blades, but dueling in the traditional manner with non-lethal blades is still a valuable and fascinating lesson in human interaction, the training for which not only works the physical body but the mental/emotional and perhaps the spiritual as well.

The techniques, entries, strikes, and counters needed to prevail in a duel are as numerous as the variety of opponents one can meet. Rather than go into detail about all of these aspects, this article will focus on three fundamental skills, universal in nature and particularly pertinent to sword fighting, that underlie the Corto Kadena system. These are:

1) The ability to understand relative motion and extrapolate from it.
2) The ability to be accurate.
3) The ability to differentiate a real threat from a feint.

Relative motion: the way that two people interact in an attempt to gain an advantageous position from which to strike, while maintaining a defensive wall.

Striking: involves choosing the position, angle, and timing from which a strike must be done in relation to the opponent's motion and position.

Ability to extrapolate: understanding how the human body moves over time and understanding at each moment, the available options for stepping, weight shifting, and striking.

Accuracy: refers not only to the ability to strike a chosen target, but to accuracy in judging range, differentiating angles of attack, and the ability to "catch" an opponent's rhythm.

Internalizing these concepts comes from partner practice, by watching others move in relation to oneself, and experiencing the potential actions and reactions as the motion unfolds. Understanding gained through a dynamic, free-form interaction with a partner will train the body to respond appropriately in real time by learning to recognize patterns and rhythms in movement. The Corto Kadena system trains these skills using the concepts of "pendulum motion" and "random flow." A pendulum has the quality of continuous motion. The two still points at either end of the swing come at the cusp of a deceleration and an acceleration and are only momentary. Pendulum motion ebbs and flows, gives and takes, but always re-cycles its energy.

There are three main pendulums: 1) the stepping pendulum, 2) the body pendulum, and 3) the weapon pendulum. In the beginning, the pendulums are practiced in a straight line, either with a swinging target or with a partner. The idea of moving in relation to something else is key. Accuracy in judging range, angle, and timing are trained and the changing position of the defense line in motion is explored.

Through practice, the motion becomes more natural and the pendulum becomes more free-form, circling around, changing lead, and moving side-to-side in no pre-determined pattern. The rhythm can change from slow to fast to slow again, but does not stop. This is Random Flow Training.

 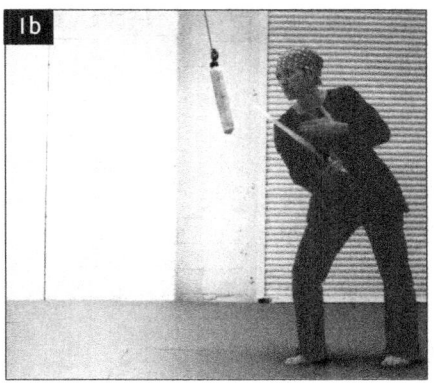

1-a-b Weapon Pendulum: The weapon extends away from and back to the body. Also practiced side-to-side. *All photos courtesy of Maija Soderholm.*

At this point, more subtle skills are introduced, including mirroring an opponent's movement (*salamin*), shadowing behind a strike (*anino*), and the use of body language to open the defensive line (*hata*).

Random Flow training is done at varying speeds, increasing with skill level. However, even highly skilled players practice at slow speeds to explore new angles, entries, and counters. The ability to keep continuous motion and accuracy of strike angle at low speed without stops, hesitations, or tracking will increase understanding of motion in real time.

Ideally, a videotape of a slow speed flow put on fast forward will look natural and real. Practicing at slow speed will also help with blade and body expression—a key element of successful feinting—and also with balance; hence the ability to issue power at any moment by exploring ways to coil and uncoil the body using high/low, left/right, and turning motions.

Like good conversation, Random Flow training is an interaction between two people where one speaks and the other listens and reacts dependent on what the first has said. This give and take will open up new angles of inquiry and new ideas to explore. The more open one is to another's questions, the more one is likely to learn.

Of course, dueling is different. It is competitive and non-cooperative. Flow, if any, happens before contact, after which the end game follows soon after. However, if our goal is to prevail in such an interaction, it is well worth our while to "converse" as widely as possible in our training, for the only true knowledge is experience. Training the eyes to see things for what they truly are, to evaluate the novel and unexpected, and respond appropriately is the best way to stay alive.

TECHNICAL SECTION

2-a-c Body Pendulum: The weight shifts from one leg to the other, forward and backward as shown. Shifting can also be side-to-side.

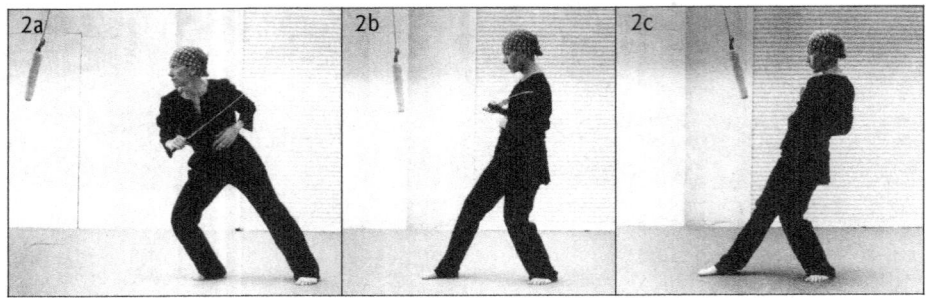

3-a-c Stepping Pendulum: Stepping pivots the body 180 degrees. For a Right Side Pendulum, the left foot stays as a fixed point and the right foot moves (opposite for Left Side Pendulum). The weight stays on the balls of the feet to facilitate pivoting. A change in direction can be executed from the central or neutral position (3-b), to encompass all 360 degrees of movement. Note how the opponents mirror each other's movement. The ability to syncopate these three pendulums is a key skill in flow training.

4-a-d The Defense Line in Motion: An understanding of how to maintain a defensive "wall" relative to a moving opponent means one can stay in range longer instead of backing away out of range and having to re-enter.

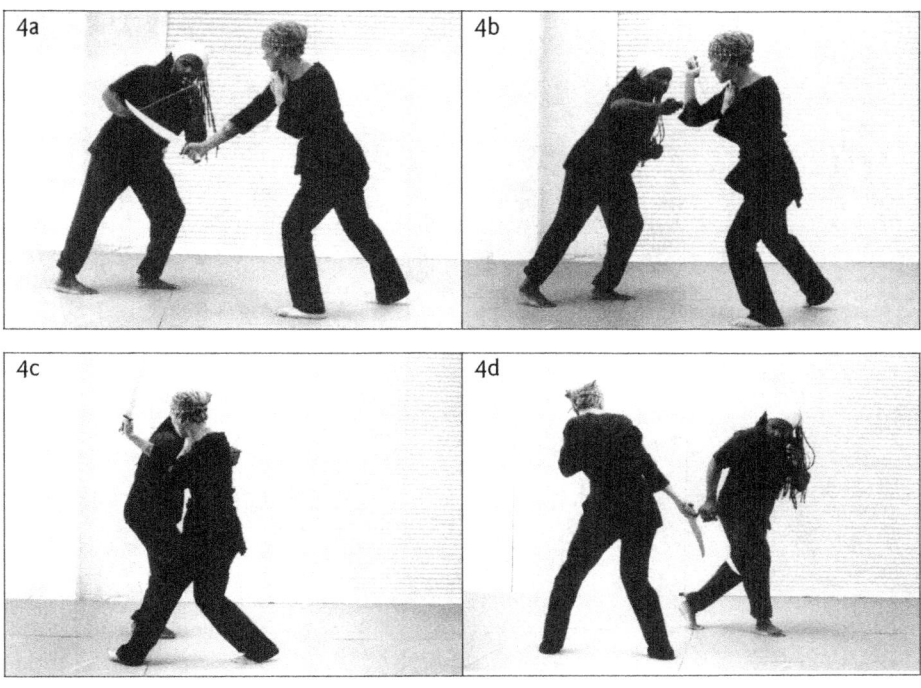

5-a-d-c "Mirroring" (salamin):
By mirroring an opponent's blade and body angle, one protects the targets closest to their blade position, thus closing the most accessible targets they are in a position to strike.

6-a-e "Shadowing" (anino): By adding the subtlety of timing to mirroring, one can "slip" an opponent's strike and enter behind their defensive line.

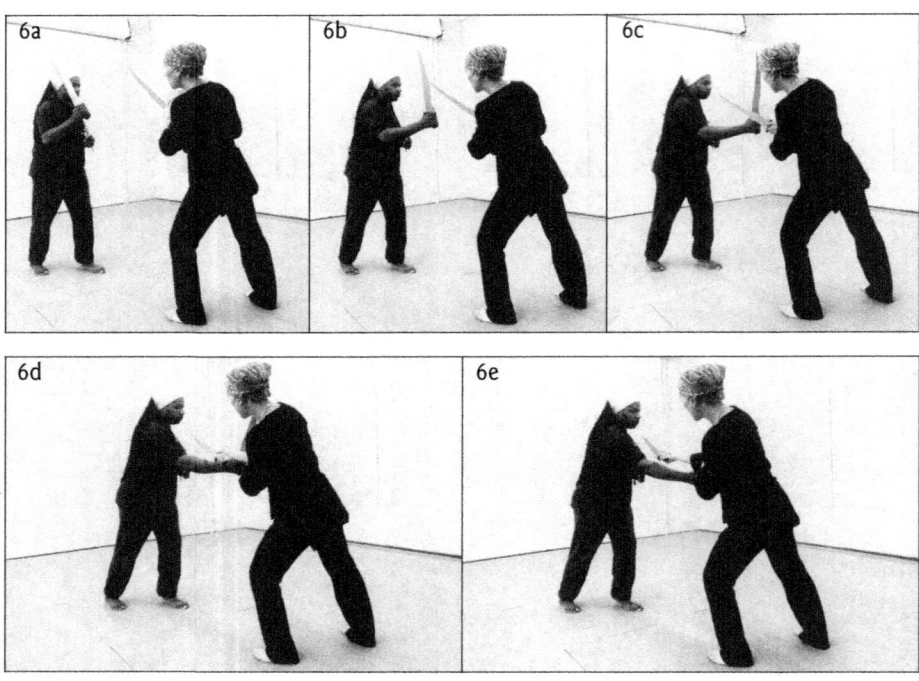

7-a-d "Feinting" (hata):

Feinting requires a "feed" to cause the opponent to respond. If the response creates our opening, one can recreate the same feed later with the body, however, this time using a strike angle aimed at the opening. In the sequence above, a threat to the opponent's sword arm causes an overextended block to the right. Later, the same body angle is fed, however the blade is now directed at the opening on the left side.

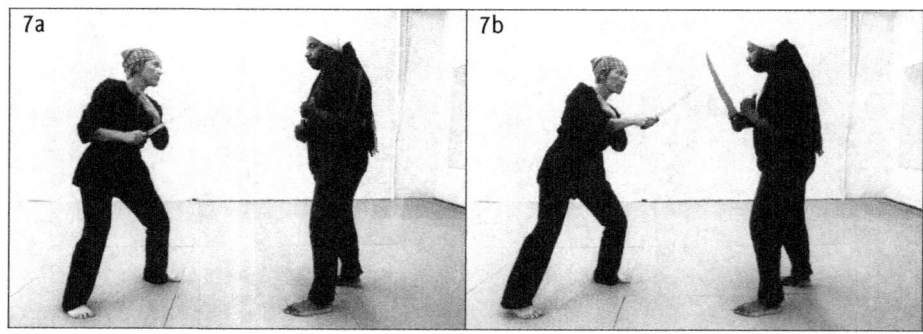

8-a-d Feinting Variation: Feinting can also draw the opponent into making an attack, thus making an opening. An overly long cut invites a strike to the right ribs. Once the opponent has committed, a pivot out of range creates an opening for a cut to the underside of their weapon arm.

9-a-e Coiling To Issue Power: In the previous sequence (8-a-d), a pivot combined with a weight shift to the back creates a powerful pulling or whipping motion. The power is created by stepping behind and pivoting on both feet, creating an unwinding motion through the body and accelerating the blade.

10-a-j

Random Flow
"Conversation"

ACKNOWLEDGMENT

A special thanks to Kenneth Ingram for appearing in the technical section with the author.

· 6 ·

The Ki to a Lasting Marriage: The Application of Internal Martial Arts Principles in the Marital Dojo

by Richard Vogel, Ph.D.

Drawings are from the first in a
graphic novel series by Oscar Ratti and
Adele Westbrook titled: *Tales of the Hermit*.
© 2001 Futuro Designs and Publications.

Marriage is hard work, as proven by the fact that the divorce rate in America is approaching fifty percent. According to retired Princeton University family historian Lawrence Stone, "The scale of marital breakdowns in the West has no historical precedent" (Bander, 2004: 60). As a psychologist who has specialized in marital therapy for twenty years, I have found that the application of the practice and the metaphysical underpinnings of internal martial arts systems can restore and perpetuate goodwill between embattled spouses. The energetic principles of taiji, aikido, and the ageless wisdom of the *Yijing* (Book of Changes; *I Ching*) are readily applicable to the tumultuous conditions intrinsic to the marital dojo.

Embroiled spouses may want a more lasting and satisfying relationship, but they often find it hard to, in *Yijing* terminology, "meet their partner halfway." As in martial arts practice, where rigidity of response predicts one's own uprooting, so too in the marital arena, defensiveness and a refusal to yield precludes harmonious interactions, contributes to marital disaffection, and can lead to the finality of divorce. The havoc and heartache couples and their children suffer in the aftermath of a divorce make it imperative that spouses acquire skills that will enable them to regulate their emotions and maintain harmonious relations.

In his book *Tai Chi According to the Yi Jing*, Stuart Olson emphasizes the universality and transferability of taiji practice to the challenges that we face in our daily lives. He comments (2001: 13):

> Another aspect of [taiji] practice is the development of wisdom, or mental accomplishment. When a person focuses his or her mind on the principles of Yielding, Relaxing, Adhering, and so on, these aspects then, over time, also become part of the person's temperament, bringing forth a more tranquil and less aggressive response to the obstacles in life.

In a similar vein, Koichi Tohei in *Aikido in Daily Life* conveys a similar sentiment (1996: 17):

> Just training at the training hall and being able to apply techniques to our opponents is not the entire great road of the universal... Of course, training hall practice is important, but it is not the only method. One only knows true Aikido... when he applies the principles of Aikido to everything he does.

Conflicts between partners are bound to arise in marriage because no two people are exactly alike. Differences of opinion, beliefs, and temperament do not imply incompatibility—nor does similarity of viewpoint and temperament guarantee smooth sailing. Partners who are tolerant of one another's differences are more likely to experience greater mutual affection than are partners who berate and coerce one another to conform to their personal points of view. According to psychologist Erich Fromm, the very process of resolving conflict fosters resiliency in each of the partners and contributes to a more intimate relationship. "Real conflicts between two people . . . are not destructive. They lead to clarification, they produce a catharsis from which both persons emerge with more knowledge and more strength" (Fromm, 1956: 93).

Drawing from the *Yijing's* vast reservoir of wisdom, Carol Anthony writes, "enduring stressful situations seems to be the only way we can transform what we have learned through the intellect into knowledge of the heart." She explains that the hexagram Taming Power of the Great refers to the repeated practice of finding our way through stressful situations as practicing "chariot driving" (Anthony, 1998: 115). In the hexagram Obstruction, we are counseled that "an obstruction that lasts only for a time is useful for self-development. This is the value of adversity" (Baynes, 1967: 153). Each of these hexagrams reminds embattled couples that the stressors to our daily life, including those of the marital dojo, provide an opportunity for inner enrichment and education.

Marital partners in conflict often assume a defensive posture when they are on the receiving end of their spouses' accumulated resentments. During such times, it is extremely difficult to maintain one's composure. Rather than give one's partner the benefit of the doubt, the tendency is to dismiss their concerns and counter-complain. Such defensiveness inflames an already worsening scenario and impedes reconciliation. In an atmosphere fueled by resentment, devoid of even the remnants of goodwill that once existed, feuding spouses typically denigrate one another's intent and impugn the other's character. "You always…" or "You never…" are the distorted versions of reality that spouses attribute to one another in the heat of battle. Such comments are demoralizing, increase frustration, and, if kept up indefinitely, engender the "moment of fatal peril," a nomenclature referred to in anger management groups that describes marital partners escalating conflict to the point of physical or verbal abuse. An example of such a tragic outcome was quoted recently in a local newspaper:

> Ralph Johnson, 30, pleaded guilty in San Jose to murdering his 34-year old wife during an argument that began over what to have for dinner. "She was serving macaroni and cheese and Tater Tots, and he wanted something more healthful," defense lawyer Stanley Golden said. "And it grew into an argument over everything in their lives. They fought off and on through the evening, and finally, shortly before midnight, he strangled her in the bathroom as she was getting ready to take a bath."

Tohei draws constructive advice for couples from his aikido practice, the application of which might have effectively helped Mr. Johnson to prevent the fatal outcome. "If you realize that, whatever happens, whatever your wife says to you, this is the time to practice the single spot, not only will you keep your temper, you will actually make a great deal of progress. If you practice the single spot only at the training hall and lose it when you get home, you have wasted your effort" (Tohei, 1996: 161).

This disaster may also have been averted if Mr. Johnson had known and consulted the *Yijing*. Its advice in a hexagram called The Abysmal is applicable to and might have prevented this fatal outcome:

> The abyss is not filled to overflowing.
> It is filled only to the rim.
> No blame.

These lines are interpreted as follows: "…Danger comes because one is too ambitious… a man when in danger has only to proceed along the line of least resistance; thus he reaches the goal. Great labors cannot be accomplished in such times; it is enough to get out of the danger" (Baynes, 1967: 117).

The *Yijing*'s underlying Daoist imperative cautions that, when we experience intense emotions that, if acted upon, would threaten our own or a loved one's well being, we can, for the time being, overcome the immediate danger by showing restraint. To aspire to anything more than the immediate cessation of hostility would, according to the *Yijing*, be foolhardy and in this instance could have contributed to this fatal outcome.

John Gottman, a leading marriage researcher and author of *Seven Principles for Making Marriage Work*, indicates that 81 percent of marriages fail when men refuse to accept their wives' influence. "Our study didn't really find that men should give up all of their personal power and let their wives rule their lives," Gottman writes.

> But we did find that the happiest, most stable marriages in the long run were those where the husband treated his wife with respect and did not resist power sharing and decision making with her.
> – Gottman, 2000: 101

The *Yijing* offers sage advice regarding the virtue of accepting a wife's influence in its commentary in the hexagram Resoluteness/Breakthrough. It advises that "if a man were to let himself be led, but not like a sheep, remorse would disappear" (Baynes, 1967: 169). Both Gottman and the *Yijing* are quick to point out that receptivity to and the acceptance of our partner's influence is not to be confused with subservience. Men usually resist meeting their partners halfway because they misconstrue accepting influence as a sign of weakness. On the contrary, the ability to accept one's partner's influence is a sign of strength and the mark of a courageous, flexible man.

One avid taiji practitioner, who desires harmonious relations in his marriage, views Gottman's recommendation regarding accepting a wife's influence as analogous to the yielding principle intrinsic to daily taiji practice. When applied to the marital arena, the yielding principle teaches us to substitute an adversarial response with one that is more receptive to our partner's concerns. By resisting the temptation proffered by our cantankerous mind to selfishly place one's own needs above those of a partner, a couple can ward off susceptibility to marital disaffection that typically presages divorce and enjoy feelings of tenderness and respect.

George Leonard, noted aikido practitioner and educator, alludes to this dynamic in marriage. "The ability to surrender to your art is a mark of the master, whether the art is martial or marital…. Are you willing at times to yield totally on some long-standing dispute for the sake of growth and change in your relationship?" (Leonard, 1991: 149).

To aspire to harmonious interactions with one's partner requires a consideration of and accommodation to their point of view. This outcome is predicated upon our ability to listen attentively to our partner's concerns. Psychologists, spiritual teachers, and ancient sages agree on the importance of listening. According to Gottman, "the better able you are to listen to what your spouse has to say and to consider her perspective respectfully, the more likely it is that you'll be able to come up with a solution or approach to a problem that satisfies you both. If your ears are closed to your spouse's needs, opinions, and values, compromise just doesn't have a chance" (Gottman, 1995: 438).

The listening that Gottman refers to is non-defensive and non-reactive. While not easy to do, non-defensive listening conveys one's fascination with an opinion or belief that differs from one's own. In a similar vein, Thich Nhat Hanh, renowned Buddhist teacher, advises: "Listening with compassion can help the other person to suffer less…. The other person might be our father, our son, our daughter, or our partner. Learning to listen to the other person can really help her to transform her anger and suffering" (Thich, 2001: 4).

Martial arts practice hones our skill at listening. In his book *Tai-Chi Ch'üan Its Effects and Practical Applications*, Yearning K. Chen (Chen, 1957: 7) identifies "auditive energy" (*ting jin*) as a sensitivity to one's training partner that can be developed through diligent practice of the taiji solo form and various two-person practices such as push hands and *dalu*. The cultivation of this unusual form of sensitivity enhances self-development, push hands practice and is conducive to a more harmonious relationship with significant others such as one's spouse and children. The auditive energy that Chen refers to is certainly applicable to the marital dojo. It implies a receptivity to the energy field of one's partner, an enhanced sensitivity to the expression of their authentic concerns and the incentive to validate rather than respond defensively to what one's partner is saying.

Aikido practitioner and psychologist Richard Heckler views the marital domain as analogous to partners training in the dojo. For Heckler, the skill of listening is a fully embodied sentiment that is conveyed in the entirety of one's being. "To move effectively with one's partner through change requires the skill of listening. Listening requires a body that is present, open, and connected. It means quieting the internal noise about how you think things should be and blend with the concerns of the other" (Heckler, 1997: 77).

Aikido's "blending" principle mirrors the auditive energy that Chen refers to. By harmonizing with one's opponent, who for the moment and in the midst of gridlock may be one's spouse, the experience of being a combatant disappears and is replaced by a friend who is working with us, not against us.

These esoteric energetic principles of martial arts and the *Yijing* can and should be applied to the domain of interpersonal relations that include marriage and child rearing. By transferring the heightened awareness and enhancement of energy that is an outcome of one's daily practice to the marital relationship, we become a source of inspiration to our spouse rather than an opponent, increasing the likelihood that our marriages will endure and prosper.

A Living Scenario

The true case of Frank and his transformation from malevolent husband and parent to harmonious benefactor exemplifies the power of bringing the wisdom of these arts into our marriages. Frank is a motivated taiji practitioner and also meditates. He awakens at five AM, meditates for an hour and then begins his taiji and qigong practice. In the aftermath of these activities, he feels energized and confident. He likes to think of himself as someone who is generous in spirit, and responsive to the needs of others. To people in the outside world, he expresses all of these virtues. Unfortunately, Frank's wife is not the recipient of the "mensch" mentality that he brings to everyone but his spouse. In relation to his nuclear family and his wife in particular, he is at times more of an ogre than benefactor.

For example, in his taiji practice, Frank takes pride in his ability to hold the meditative Universal Post posture (*Yuju Cong*) for over an hour, an example of his carefully honed patience and inner calm. Unfortunately, he does not transfer his patience to his wife and children, with whom he is often irritable and impatient. This is upsetting to his wife.

While Frank will go beyond the call of duty to help others outside his family, at home he reacts defensively and often minimizes the concerns of his wife, Marie, around housekeeping and the care of their children. She is impeccable in both domains. Rather then construe her fastidiousness in relation to the upkeep of their home and the needs of their children as beneficial to his family, Frank trivializes her concerns and encourages a *laissez faire* attitude. Marie wants Frank to show her the consideration of cleaning up after himself and not behaving in a slovenly manner. When Frank washes the dishes, he is careless, leaving bits of food on the plates. He begins household projects only to leave them unfinished. Marie attempts to be tolerant of Frank's deficiency in this arena, but she's frustrated at not having more of her needs met. Frank's threshold for a chaotic environment is much greater than his wife's and, while they attempt to compromise in this domain, Frank's wife often feels that she gets the short end of the stick.

Along with his taiji practice, Frank is a student of Buddhism, particularly its emphasis on mindfulness in daily life. Recently, Frank achieved a breakthrough in his understanding of how his defensiveness has been corrosive to his marriage after reading a passage from Thich Nhat Hanh's book *Anger* (2001). Thich is both a poet and an avid gardener. Friends counseled him to abandon the vegetable garden so he could write more poetry. Thich replied that from the Buddhist point of view, it is important to be mindful in all activities in the course of one's day, be they mundane or esoteric. One does not take precedence over the other. "You cannot just sit there and write the story or the novel," Thich comments. "You have to do other things as well. You drink tea, cook breakfast, wash your clothes, water the vegetables.... You have to do them well" (Thich, 2001: 201).

Leonard (1991: 150) compliments Thich's statement regarding the transferability of skills acquired in the course of refining one's art to other and what might be erroneously thought of as more mundane endeavors as follows:

> ... the principles of mastery can guide you whatever skill you seek to develop, whatever path you choose to walk... Ultimately, nothing in this life is 'commonplace,' nothing is 'in between.' The threads that join your every act, your every thought, are infinite. All paths of mastery eventually merge.

Thich's words inspired Frank to respond more empathetically to his wife's concerns. He no longer ignores the discrepancy that exists between the rigor that he applies to his martial art and his utter abandonment of his household responsibilities. He recognizes that he whole-heartedly applies himself to his martial arts practice, with the aim of excelling in his art. Now he is committed to applying to his marriage the same standards of excellence and mindfulness that he does to his martial arts practice. His goal is to become as exquisitely attuned to his wife and children as he is to applying the techniques and aesthetics of his taiji practice. Frank now respects Marie's fastidiousness in the upkeep of their home as parallel to the way in which he continuously refines his own art. These days, during his early morning practice, as he holds the Universal Post posture, Frank reflects on Thich's commentary, "Enlightenment is not separate from washing dishes or growing lettuce. To learn how to live each moment of our daily life in deep mindfulness and concentration is the practice" (Thich, 2001: 202).

Closing Comments

My intent in writing this chapter has been to encourage the reader to impart to his wife and children the benefits, both martial and meditative, that have accrued as a result of his diligent practice of his art. It is to the entire family's benefit to have a more confident and serene husband and father in their midst.

Psychologists prescribe a *time out* regimen for feuding spouses to prevent further harm from being done to their relationship. The time out is an occasion for inner enrichment where each spouse independently of the other, is encouraged to supplant agitation and rancor with a more relaxed and sanguine response.

I know of no more efficient time out and self-soothing elixir than the repetition of a few rounds of taiji. The repetition of these graceful movements dignifies all of one's actions so that one is disinclined to harbor resentment towards one's spouse in the aftermath of a disagreement. The *Yijing* refers to the resumption of good will between formerly disaffected spouses as "the return of understanding after an estrangement" where "everything must be treated tenderly and with care at the beginning, so that the return may lead to a flowering" (Baynes, 1967: 98).

A favorable rapprochement, such as that which occurred for Frank and Marie in the example cited above, is a predictable outcome for the martial arts practitioner who embodies in the totality of his actions the underlying tenets of his art.

Dedication: I dedicate this article to my wife and training partner Tracy Rose—my inspiration.

Bibliography

Anthony, C. (1998). *The philosophy of the I Ching.* Stow, MA: Anthony Publishing.

Bander, B. (2004). *Love that works.* Philadelphia: Templeton Foundation Press.

Baynes, W. (1967). *The I Ching or book of changes.* Princeton, NJ: Princeton University Press.

Chen, Y. (1957). *Tai-chi chuan: It's effects and practical applications.* Hong Kong: n.p.

Fromm, E. (1956). *The art of loving.* New York: Harper and Row.

Gottman, J. (2000). *Seven principles for making marriage work.* Santa Clarita, CA: Crown Publishing.

Gottman, J. (1996). *What predicts divorce.* Mahwah, NJ: Erlbaum Lawrence Associates.

Leonard, G. (1991). *Mastery.* New York: Penguin Books.

Olson, S. (2001). *Tai-chi according to the I Ching.* Rochester, VT: Inner Traditions.

Thich, N. (2001). *Anger.* New York: Riverhead Books.

Tohei, K. (1996). *Aikido in daily life.* Tokyo: Rikugei Publishing.

· 7 ·

North Korean Kyu Sun Hui: An Extraordinary Olympic Judo Player

by David Finch

All photos courtesy of Judo Photos Unlimited.

At the 1996 Atlanta Olympics, North Korean Kye Sun Hui became the youngest gold medallist in Olympic Judo history at the age of sixteen. As a 'wild card' chosen by the International Judo Federation (IJF), she astonishingly defeated Japan's Tamura Ryoko (Tani) with a with a sweeping hip counter (*harai-goshi-gaeshi*). Afterwards Kye cheekily said: "It is easier to fight in international tournaments abroad than it is to fight at home," referring to the strong domestic opposition.

Kye defeats Japan's Tamura Ryoko at the 1996 Atlanta Olympics.

Until her defeat in Atlanta, Tamura had been unbeaten in 84 contests and was universally expected to take the title. In fact, until Atlanta, Kye had never fought outside North Korea, was entirely unknown, and didn't even know who Tamura was until the day they met. That proved to be a distinct psychological advantage to the North Korean who later stood on the podium draped in the North Korean flag.

By the time of the Paris World Judo Championships a year later in 1997, she was at a weight heavier class (52 kgs, or 115 lbs) and won the silver medal, losing to France's Marie-Claire Restoux. Kye lost momentum at the 1999 Birmingham World Judo Championships and could only manage a bronze medal, repeating this at the Sydney Olympics where she lost the semifinal to Cuba's Legna Verdecia, the eventual gold medallist. At the age of twenty, Kye appeared to be fading rapidly. However, the 2001 Munich Worlds Championships re-established her reputation when she defeated Germany's Rafaella Imbriani in the final, again in the 52 kgs (115 lbs) class.

Above: Germany's Rafaella Imbriani gets defeated by Kye in the final Munich World Championships, 2001. **Below:** Kye employs a major hip throw (*ogoshi*) to defeat Germany's Yvonne Boenisch in the finals of the Osaka World Championships, 2003.

With extreme precision, Kye caught Boenisch with an inner-thigh throw to claim her third world title in just 38 seconds at the Cairo World Championships, 2005.

Two years later at the Osaka World Championships in 2003, she moved up to the 57 kgs (125.4 lbs) weight class. There she stormed through the opposition winning every contest by *ippon* (equivalent to a knockout), including the final against Germany's Yvonne Boenisch. In response, her opponents could only manage minor technical points against her—such was the intensity of her style. In the final, Kye led Boenisch by a strong lead in points until fifteen seconds from the bell. Then Kye unleashed an explosive major hip throw (*ogoshi*) that resulted in a winning ippon. Trying to avoid the score with an outstretched arm, Boenisch dislocated her elbow. But not a scream came from her even though she was in great pain.

Nearly a year later in 2004, Kye and Boenisch met again in the 57kgs (125.4 lbs) final of the Athens Olympics. Boenisch was better prepared and this time turned the tables on Kye. She had fought Kye earlier in the year at the final of the Warsaw 'A' tournament where she had defeated her. Now, fully aware of Kye's style, Boenisch proved too awkward for her, never giving her time to settle into the fight, thus ensuring that Kye could not use her favourite grip. Boenisch comprehensively outwitted her and then scored with an inner-thigh throw (*uchimata*) while Kye was warned for passivity, resulting in a particularly satisfying tactical victory for Boenisch.

At the recent Cairo World Championships, held in September of 2005, both Kye and Boenisch were destined to meet again for their third major finals confrontation. Unlike the Osaka World Championships, Kye reached the final having finished only one contest with an ippon inside the five minutes. That is until she met Cuba's Yurisle Lupetey in the semi-final.

Leading by five points, Kye unleashed a determined attack that resulted in Lupetey being carried off in a stretcher with a broken elbow just like Boenisch's at Osaka. One spectator who saw the throw at close quarters, Rusty Kanokogi of the IJF, said: "When force met force, something had to give. Kye was determined to throw Lupetey through the mat, but the Cuban was not going to give away a score resulting in her elbow giving way while attempting to avoid an ippon loss." The break was so painful that the Cuban was unable to stop screaming while receiving attention.

The final was not a repetition of what happened in Osaka. This was a far more convincing win for Kye against Boenisch. Now firing on all cylinders, Kye attacked with an inner-thigh throw (uchimata). Boenisch resisted the threat, but not the next. With extreme precision, Kye caught Boenisch perfectly with a second inner-thigh throw to claim her third world title in just 38 seconds. The win caused the small gathering of North Korean spectators to go wild with joy.

In North Korea, Kye is the "People's Athlete" and has been given the title of a "Labor Heroine of the Democratic People's Republic of Korea." She was also given a special award by the late Kim Il Sung, founder of that state.

When Kye returned from Cairo, North Korean Television reported that about 100,000 people turned out to welcome her with bouquets, slogan boards, drums, cymbals, and confetti, reminiscent of a New York "ticker tape" welcome. The television station reported that she had said that current leader Kim Jong Il had given her "strength, courage, matchless guts, and resolution," attributing her success to what she called Kim's "unbounded love and trust." In a freer society, such gifts are more likely to be attributed to God than a politician. But certainly she is highly gifted and, at 26-years of age, still has time to receive more judo titles, and sporting accolades from leader Kim Jong Il.

Judo Weight Classes

Extra lightweight:
Men -60kg, Women -48kg

Half lightweight:
Men -66kg, Women -52kg

Lightweight:
Men -73kg, Women -57kg

Half-middleweight:
Men -81kg, Women -63kg

Middleweight:
Men -90kg, Women -70kg

Half-heavyweight:
Men -100kg, Women -78kg

Heavyweight:
Men +100kg, Women +78kg

· 8 ·

The Maiden of Yue:
Fount of Chinese Martial Arts Theory

by Stanley E. Henning, M.A.

The Maiden of Yue parry's Old Yuan's thrust.

Chinese martial arts theory is based on Daoist philosophical concepts that form a major element of the Chinese worldview, a worldview held prior to the establishment of the formal Daoist religion. The earliest and still most complete yet concise exposition of this theory is found in the story of the Maiden of Yue, related in the *Spring and Autumn Annals of the Kingdoms of Wu and Yue* (written during the Eastern Han, 25-220 C.E., about the Kingdoms of Wu and Yue, during the latter part of the Spring and Autumn period, ca. 560-476 B.C.E.) (Zhang, 1994: 366-370).

The significance of the story of the Maiden of Yue to our understanding of Chinese martial arts history and practice is such that—even in the face of the sometimes obscure and ambiguous nature of classical Chinese writings and resultant potential for mistranslation, not only into other languages but into modern Chinese as well—it is worth the effort to meet the challenge and attempt to render a more accurate translation of this important passage than I have seen to date.

Gou Jian, King of Yue (497-465 B.C.E.), with his seat of power in Shaoxing, Zhejiang, sought revenge for an earlier defeat inflicted by the King of Wu, whose center of power was in neighboring Jiangsu. Gou Jian spent considerable time and effort to insure victory against the King of Wu. His preparations included the best possible training for his army in hand-to-hand combat skills. According to the story, Gou Jian's trusted advisor, Fan Li, recommended he seek to employ a young woman widely known in the kingdom for her sword fighting skills to train his key combat leaders.

Upon receipt of the notice to report for an audience with the king, the young woman began the several day trek to the capital of Yue. As the story goes, she met an elderly man en route in an isolated forest area. He introduced himself as Old Yuan, commented that he had heard of the young woman's sword fighting fame, and asked her to demonstrate her skill for him. The young women politely assented and invited Old Yuan to test her. Old Yuan thereupon broke off a length of dry bamboo, from which a shorter tip snapped off in the process. The young woman let Old Yuan thrust at her three times. After Old Yuan's third try, she picked up the broken bamboo tip and struck in at him, upon which he jumped up into a tree and was transformed into a white ape. With this test of her skill from an encounter with a supernatural being, the young woman took leave of the white ape and continued her journey to meet the King of Yue.

When he met the young woman, the King of Yue asked her two questions: (1) what kind of sword technique was it that she practiced—where did it come from?; and (2), what was the theory upon which her sword technique was based? As to the first question, she replied:

> This little girl [1] was born deep in the mountains and dense forest, and grew up in the unpopulated wilds without a place to study or practice, and I had no association with the nobility. I did not learn from others, but practiced alone and suddenly it came to me.

Her answer to the second question was as follows:

> The theory is very subtle yet easy to understand. Its true significance is hidden and deep. The theory includes both large [double/offense] and small [single/defense] doors, and *yin* [passive/yielding] and *yang* [active/attacking] aspects. Open the large door and close the small one [move from the defense to

the offense], passivity recedes and activity rises.[1] The following precepts are applicable to all forms of hand-to-hand combat: strengthen the spirit within, appear calm without; give the appearance of a proper woman and fight like an aroused tiger; generate energy throughout your body and move with your spirit; remain distant and obscure as the sun,[2] and quick and agile as a bounding hare; now your opponent sees you [chases your form], now he doesn't [pursues your shadow], and the sword blade flashes similarly; breathe with movement and do not break the rules; side-to-side, back-and-forth, direct attack or reverse blow, the opponent does not hear these [your movements are not telegraphed].[3] This body of theory will allow one person to resist one hundred and a hundred to resist ten thousand.

Gou Jian, King of Yue (497-465 B.C.E.), with his seat of power in Shaoxing, Zhejiang, was impressed with the young woman's explanations and is said to have arranged for her to teach his key combat leaders so that they, in turn could further train their troops. In addition, he bestowed upon her the title, Maiden of Yue, by which she was known ever after.

While the story may be apocryphal (the white ape portion, as a minimum, is merely symbolic), the martial arts theory presented is genuine. My translation attempts to remain true to the intent of the subject matter. The most obvious point made in this passage is that the precepts listed are applicable to all forms of hand-to-hand combat. At the time this was written there was no categorization of Chinese martial arts into Internal and External schools, a concept that was first postulated in 1669 in Huang Zongxi's *Epitaph for Wang Zhengnan* (an artificial construct with possible political connotations (Henning, 1997: 10-19). The majority of this piece consists of supporting information—the actual Epitaph is only one line long and does not contain the terms Internal or External. No specific Internal styles beyond the Internal School itself in the Epitaph were named until the late 19th century to the early 20th.

Regardless of this artificial categorization of Chinese martial arts into Internal and External schools, the precepts enumerated by the Maiden of Yue consist of both Internal and External aspects common to all the martial arts. To attempt to separate these complementary aspects into competing schools is artificial and strays from the "hidden and deep significance" of original Chinese martial arts theory. In this respect, it is significant that only three styles of boxing—taijiquan, xingyiquan, and baguazhang—have ever been specifically named as representing the so-called Internal School of Chinese martial arts. However, rather than considering them as belonging to the Internal School of martial arts, it would be more appropriate to identify them as ideal representatives of traditional Chinese martial arts theory first described in the story of the Maiden of Yue.

Glossary

- *bai yuan:* white ape   白猿
- *damen:* large door/stance   大門
- *menhu:* door, also means "factions," but may also refer to offense and defense in the martial arts.   門戶
- *xiaomen:* (small door/stance)   小門
- *yao:* (distant/obscure)   杳
- *Yuan Gong:* (Old Yuan). The surname, *Yuan*, is pronounced the same as *yuan*, meaning ape.   袁公
- *Yuennü:* Maiden of Yue   越女

Notes

[1] The Chinese term is the combination *menhu*, *men* meaning double swinging (large) door and *hu* meaning single (small) door. One can find a number of meanings for this term in any dictionary; however, I think the meaning here, related to the martial arts, is not found in any dictionary I know of, so I interpret *men* as referring to the offensive or attack mode, and *hu* as referring to the defensive mode. Without the benefit of further explanation, I question Zhang Jue's colloquial Chinese translation of the passage, "Open the large door and close the small one" as roughly reading "Open the door to the correct path, and block the harmful door and false way" (Zhang, 1994: 369). This seems to give an unwarranted negative connotation to the term *menhu* (door) and, by association, the *yin* (yielding) and *yang* (attacking) balance. However, this passage could merely mean, "Don't stray from the basic principles" or words to that effect. On the other hand, I feel that the term "*menhu*" might possibly represent the earliest expression of a broader concept from which the narrower concept of attacking (direct facing) and defensive (sideways) stances evolved by the Ming period (1368-1644). This narrower concept can be seen in General Yu Dayou's (1503-1579) *Sword Classic*,

where *damen* (large door) represents the attacking (direct facing) stance and *xiaomen* (small door) represents the defensive (sideways facing) stance. Thus, the ultimate meaning of *menhu* in the Maiden of Yue story remains open to interpretation.

2   My translation describes the martial artist as "distant and obscure as the sun," based on the definition of the Chinese character *yao*, which is formed by combining the characters for tree (*mu*) and sun (*ri*)—or simplistically explained as viewing the sun through the trees. The sun may appear bright in the sky, but this by no means makes its inherent characteristics any less mysterious. In a like manner, the martial artist may appear to be like anyone else, but protects the secrets of his techniques. Or, as Ge Hong (283-363 C.E.) noted, the martial arts all have their secrets and if one fights another who does not know them he can be victorious (Ge, 1997: 987).

   I am aware that my translation differs significantly on this point from that of Douglas Wile in his book, *T'ai Chi's Ancestors*. Wile translates this passage as, "Your skill should be as obvious as the sun and as startling as a bolting hare" (Wile, 1999: 4). The difference appears to be due to differing interpretations of the meaning of the character *yao*.

3   Wile translates this passage as, "Whether you close with the opponent vertically or horizontally, with or against the flow, never attack frontally" (Wile, 1999: 4). Nowhere do I see an admonition against a frontal attack in the Maiden of Yue text—only that one should attack in a manner that is not detected by an opponent.

Bibliography

Ge Hong (1997). *Complete translation of the "Baopuzi external chapters."* Pang Yueguang, (Tr.). Guiyang: Guizhou People's Press.

Henning, S. (1997). Chinese boxing: The internal versus external schools in the light of history and theory. *Journal of Asian Martial Arts*, (6)3: 10-19.

Wile, D. (1999). *T'ai chi's ancestors: The making of an internal martial art*. New York: Sweet Ch'i Press.

Xu Zhen (1936). *Record of investigation into the facts on taijiquan*. Taibei: Zhen-shan-mei Press, 1965.

Yu Dayou (1988). "Sword classic," in Qi Jiguang, (c. 1561) *New book of effective discipline*, juan 12, Ma Mingda, (Ed.). Beijing: People's Physical Culture Press, 250-280.

Zhang Jue (Tr.) (1994). *Complete translation of the Spring and Autumn Annals of Wu and Yue*, waijuan 9, Zhao Hua (Later Han). Guiyang: Guizhou People's Press.

· 9 ·

Fighting Women of Kabuki Theater and the Legacy of Women's Japanese Martial Arts

by Deborah Klens-Bigman, Ph.D.*

Ghost of Takao.

"These two swords are my husband's soul,
and when I wear them I speak for us both,
for I come as his deputy."

– Tonase, wife of samurai Kakogawa Honzo.
Quote from *The Treasury of Loyal Retainers* (Keene, 1971: 134)

Imagine the scene—a female character, her face painted a delicate white, clad in a graceful kimono, stands defiant, her husband's long and short swords thrust through her sash. Before the scene comes to a close, she will have need of them as she fights, defending her family's honor. The scene is from the play *The Treasury of Loyal Retainers* (*Kanadehon Chushingura*), a puppet play (*bunraku*) written in 1748 that was quickly adapted to the kabuki stage. It is still performed in both kabuki and bunraku theaters today.

Kabuki, the traditional, popular theater of Japan, dates from the early Edo period (1603–1868), as the Tokugawa family began to consolidate its rule and the warrior class became the de facto rulers of the country. Kabuki theaters sprang up in the three large cities of Edo (Tokyo), Kyoto, and Osaka, as well as in smaller towns. As popular theater, playwrights drew heavily on local news and scandals. Plays featuring forbidden love, suicide, murder, thievery, and revenge were hugely popular. Like the writers of the multifaceted series *Law & Order*, playwrights vaguely disguised the real-life details of plots and characters, not to avoid lawsuits, but to avoid crackdowns by government censors instead.

Stories about samurai figured prominently in kabuki. Audiences no doubt delighted in the idea that the members of the ruling class were just as human as the lowliest merchant. In addition, plays featuring warriors were filled with swordplay and use of other weapons, the "action movies" of the day. Whether out of simple curiosity, a sense of flattery, or some combination, and in spite of all the official prohibitions, members of the samurai class were just as likely to go to the theater as anyone else. It is because kabuki appealed to such a wide range of people in the Edo period that it is reasonable to conclude that the genre held up a sometimes cannily accurate mirror to Edo period life.

Kabuki is to this day performed by men only, a practice that began in the mid-seventeenth century, when both women and boys were banned from public stages. The move was made not so much to shield public morality (performances by both women and boys continued in private), as to protect public order and prevent the unauthorized mixing of classes (which happened anyway). The kabuki female role players, called *onnagata*, have fascinated Western theater scholars for over a hundred years, but in spite of this fascination, scholarship has only very recently begun to consider onnagata on their own terms, translating their own writings to gain some insight into their art and way of life.

Likewise, not much has been written specifically about stage fighting (*tachimawari*) in kabuki. Pronko addresses stage combat training in his article on the kabuki actor training program at the National Theater of Japan (1971), and I gave a presentation on the subject several years ago. Long a subject of fascination here, several Western scholars, including Mezur (2005), Komintz (1999), and Fujita and Shapiro (eds.) (2006) have specifically considered *onnagata*, but information on stage fighting by onnagata characters is scarce.

Think of onnagata and we think of graceful and beautiful characters, gliding across the stage, epitomizing beauty and elegance, and, frequently, tragedy. This image conjures up a *Madama Butterfly* image of Japanese femininity, and yet, the kabuki repertory is filled with frightening female demons, ghosts, and spirits, as well as brave samurai women. All of these female characters engage in fight scenes, and plays featuring these roles are still popular today. This chapter deals specifically with the depiction of martial prowess by onnagata. In it, I look at several plays in the kabuki repertory that include fighting women characters and their popularity with kabuki audiences, then and now. It is my contention that the popularity of fighting females in the theater reflected to a certain extent the experience of women of the samurai class, explaining at least in part their popularity. We can also trace a historical line between these fighting women characters and the female practitioners of Japanese martial arts of today.

In spite of several writers, such as Jones (1997) and Edgerton (2000), there is some reluctance to consider women as warriors or fighters. While it is true that men far outnumbered women as fighters, women warriors can be found across both centuries and cultures. There is evidence in Japan, though more research needs to be done, that women of the samurai class trained with weapons and were expected to aid in the defense of their homes when necessary.

The "Madama Butterfly" myth continues to thrive among the people who are in the best position to refute it. I have encountered women martial art practitioners outside Japan who consider themselves pioneers in a man's world (for interviews with women martial artists who take this point of view, see Hoppe [1997]). However, during my early training in Japan, even though the dojo I visited had mostly male students, the women practitioners were not regarded as anomalies, and in most cases, trained alongside the men. As we will see from the following examples, it could well be that the woman warrior (*onna budoka*) characters of kabuki are the "mothers" of the female warrior of today.

This paper examines fight scenes for several female role types—the courtesan, the magical spirit, the mountain witch, and the female samurai. All of the plays under consideration were written in the eighteenth century, embodying if not a social norm, then characterizations that were not entirely unfamiliar in real life to audiences at the time. The idea of a woman who might take up arms and fight was in no way an alien one to these audiences.

Dealing as they did with plots often involving members of the samurai class, fight scenes were integral to the popularity of kabuki. Actors trained with multiple "practical" weapons, such as sticks, swords, spears, knives, and glaives (bows being not very practical onstage), as well as an array of nonpractical items, such as wands, or branches of cherry and plum blossoms. Fans and umbrellas were also used as defensive weapons.

The fighting woman character does not seem to have developed until after Tokugawa edicts demanding actual, plotted plays go into effect. Karyu Sodezaki (?–1730) is credited with creating the woman warrior role type, though there is not much information available about him (Mezur, 2005: 80). In any case, he was not the only onnagata to engage in stage combat at the time. The onnagata who is considered one of the great founders of the art, Ayame Yoshizawa I (1673–1729), played a wide range of female characters throughout his long career. In his commentary on acting, the *Ayamegusa*, compiled around 1750, he devotes multiple entries to discussing the depiction of samurai women. In learning to handle a sword, for example:

> What should happen when a samurai's wife takes her short sword and lays about her? When she is surrounded by a large force... where she protects her lord's daughter, the samurai's wife should, unlikely though this may seem, be able to handle her sword more skillfully than a man can.
> – Dunn & Torigoe, 1969: 52

Ayame cautions that in engaging in fight scenes, the onnagata must all the same take extreme care not to appear too male, all the while showing himself as more than competent at fighting, should the part require it. He is best known for suggesting that the best way to maintain a sense of femininity was to behave as a woman both onstage and off, training advice that was apparently followed by at least some onnagata until the early twentieth century (Leiter, 2006: 75). While some scholars feel Ayame's advice pertains more to elegant courtesan roles (said to be his specialty), his preoccupation in his commentary with less-elegant characters suggests that the fiercer women characters were more difficult to make believable as "female" to an audience. Indeed, in Komintz's biography (1997), it is apparent that Ayame played a wide variety of roles throughout his career, including stern samurai matrons and even women who disguised themselves as men (for a worthy cause, of course). In the course of these performances, he engaged in swordplay along with other types of stage combat.

Ayame's great rival, Tatsunosuke Mizuki I (1673–1745), presented the flip side of the onnagata coin. Whereas the *Ayamegusa* stresses the importance of onnagata training from the inside out, Tatsunosuke's performances were based on commanding stage presence and physical agility. Early in his career, he gained popular acclaim by adapting a men's spear dance to onnagata style. Apparently his physicality also showed itself in martial prowess onstage (Komintz, 1997: 185). It would seem that Tatsunosuke's sense of feminine comportment hardly matched that of Ayame, but audiences did not seem to mind. Ayame and Tatsunosuke competed intensely with each other for the title "Best in Japan" until Tatsunosuke's retirement in 1704 (Komintz, 1997: 204).

We can see from the foregoing that woman warrior roles go back to the foundations of kabuki theater and continue to be popular with audiences today. Whether a maid guarding the castle with her *naginata* (glaive) or a samurai matron wearing her husband's swords in her sash as a token of authority, weapons and stage combat are in no way out of character for kabuki onnagata.

In giving examples of onnagata stage fighting, I will confine myself, where possible, to the specific scenes in which the fight takes place. I do this for brevity as well as sparing readers the twists and turns that make up much of kabuki plots. Those who are interested are encouraged to read the playscripts where available or look up plot summaries, many of which can be found online. I have seen all of the plays mentioned here, over many years of going to kabuki.

Fighting Female Spirit

The first play in which I will consider onnagata stage fighting is *Love's Snowbound Barrier Gate* (*Tsu-moru Koi Seki no To*), which premiered in 1784. Much of the original script has been lost, though research has suggested that the plot is so convoluted it may be just as well. The piece that remains, and is still performed, is a dance play (*shosagoto*) involving characters that transform themselves onstage—a technique that confounds devotees of Western theater even as it delights lovers of kabuki (Brandon & Leiter, 2002: 216–17).

Sekibei is a woodcutter and guardian of a barrier gate deep in the mountains. In spite of the cold and snow, a mysterious cherry tree stands upstage in spectacular full bloom. However, Sekibei is not who he appears to be: he is in reality Otomo no Kuronushi, a villain who is plotting to overthrow the current emperor. The audience has learned in the first scene that Kuronushi is responsible for the death of Yoshimine Yasusada, though his brother, Yoshimine Munesada, the manager of the barrier gate, is unaware of his identity.

Complicated, yes. But what concerns us here is a scene that is surprisingly more or less straightforward. Kuronushi, having had a great deal of rice wine, is dozing off, but before doing so he has vowed to cut down the mysterious tree in order to burn the wood as an offering to attract spiritual benefit to his nefarious cause. A woman dressed as a courtesan appears as if out of nowhere, and attempts, through dance, to seduce the drunken Kuronushi. She tells him her name is Sumizome. In reality, the courtesan is the spirit of the cherry tree. Her aim in confronting Kuronushi is twofold: to stop him from cutting down the tree, and to exact revenge for the killing of Yasusada, to whom she was married when she assumed human form.

The action of the dance begins as a love duet, but eventually descends into the stylized violence of stage fighting, with Kuronushi wielding his giant axe, and Sumizome using blossoming cherry branches as both practical and magical weapons.

As in most stage fighting scenes, the action takes place to the sound of clappers, in this case making a steady beat. Like in any good fight scene, the advantage keeps changing, with the climactic moment a gorgeous backbend (*ebisori*, or "shrimp curve") by Sumizome as she avoids the evil Kuronushi's axe. In the performance that I saw, the onnagata's head nearly touched the floor, eliciting gasps from the audience, shouts of approval, and spontaneous applause.

As the fight progresses, the antagonists take on more the appearance of their inner selves. Using a special compartment in the axe (and the axe blade itself as a mirror), the male style actor (*tachiyaku*) playing Kuronushi transforms his appearance into a demon with wild hair and eyes and a red tongue. Sumizome becomes less a courtesan and more of an avenging magical spirit, with free hair and a shimmering cherry-blossom-patterned kimono. The final tableau shows

Sumizome triumphant, standing over the vanquished Kuronushi, having protected the tree, avenged her husband, and defeated an evil plot against the throne, all at once.

In considering this scene, Sumizome does not fight until she is provoked. She endures numerous insults from Kuronushi, including the murder of her earthly husband—the precipitating act for her wrath is that in cutting down the cherry tree, Kuronushi would be killing her, too. She is therefore, in this case, acting in self-defense. However, as we will see, self-defense is only one reason a woman character would choose to fight.

The Fighting Courtesan

The next play under consideration is one of the most famous in the kabuki and bunraku repertories, *Yoshitsune and the Thousand Cherry Trees* (*Yoshitsune Senbon Zakura*), premiering in 1747. The plot revolves around a real historical character, Minamoto no Yoshitsune (1159–1189), a famous general of the Heike-Genji clan war (called the Gempei War, 1180–1185). Yoshitsune, through his spectacular abilities as a field general, helped bring about the defeat of the Heike clan. In so doing, however, he incurred the wrath of his older brother, Minamoto no Yoritomo (1149–1199), who became concerned that Yoshitsune, flush with battlefield success, might lift his hand against him. As a result, Yoritomo pursued Yoshitsune through the countryside, eventually catching up to him and bringing about his death (Sato, 1995: 110–113).

Though the actual conflict took place in the late Heian period, the costumes for *Yoshitsune and the Thousand Cherry Trees* reflect the time of its writing in the eighteenth century. It is one of the plays in the repertory that are always produced more or less in their entirety, a process that in kabuki takes one through both the day and the night programs, a total of about eight hours' performance time. Through a great deal of theatrical license, Yoshitsune is not only pursued by men under his brother's command, but also by the famous warriors of the Heike clan. Though they were defeated and killed in historical reality, wild plot devices are employed to suggest that they did not die, but come to harry Yoshitsune as he makes his way from hiding place to hiding place. These fictional plot twists featuring historical characters make *Yoshitsune and the Thousand Cherry Trees* one of the few kabuki plays that are almost as fun to read as to watch.

Yoshitsune's mistress, Shizuka Gozen, is the character that interests us here. She is a dancer who performed for nobility. Such performers are often depicted with swords thrust through their sashes, but Shizuka's costume in the play reflects a princess-type role, even as the style of the performance reflects that of a courtesan, a highly trained prostitute adept at dancing and singing.

At an early point in the play (Jones, 1993), agents loyal to Yoritomo have come to confront Yoshitsune. Yoshitsune's retainer, the fiery Saito Musashibo Benkei, is determined to stop them from reaching his lord, even as Yoshtisune determines that doing any violence to them would simply enrage his brother. Yoshitsune must stop Benkei, but how? Quickly Yoshitsune calls to Shizuka, orders her to enter the fray, and stop Benkei before he does serious harm. Responding immediately, Shizuka has a maid strap on her armor, grabs a naginata hanging over the doorway, and rushes out to stop the fight. The narrator, used in both puppet plays and kabuki, tells us what happens next:

> Then, taking the halberd [sic] from its hook,
> Shizuka grasps it tight beneath her arm,
> And off into the fray
> Dashes the woman warrior.
> Thus, the tale of Shizuka's exploits
> In the night raid at Horikawa
> Will be told to ages yet unborn.
> – Jones, 1993: 8

Much later in the play, Yoshitsune is puzzled by the fact that one of his retainers, Tadanobu, seems to be in two places at once. The men look identical to him, so there must be some magic at work. The false Tadanobu has been traveling as a bodyguard for Shizuka, who has been given a famous drum by Yoshitsune for safekeeping. Eager to find out who, or what, the imposter is, he gives his sword to Shizuka and asks her to find out the truth. In the scene that follows, she interrogates Tadanobu while threatening him with the sword. The false Tadanobu, in reality a magical fox, performs a series of acrobatic feats perfectly timed to dodge Shizuka's sword. He walks along the banister of a raised porch, and, at the climax of the scene, does a wonderful "shrimp curve" backbend down a flight of stairs to avoid her sword cut. Eventually, Shizuka determines Tadanobu's true identity, and the play continues from there.

As in much high-quality stage combat, verisimilitude in the use of weapons is an important element of any fight scene. It is telling that the narrator notes Shizuka takes the naginata "beneath her arm." In Tendo-ryu, a martial art form dating from the Edo period that to this day is mostly practiced by women, taking a naginata beneath one's arm is exactly the correct way to hold it, accommodating both the length of the weapon and its weight. In fight scenes generally, though they are sometimes fantastic in the extreme, basic handling of weapons by both male and female characters takes their special characteristics into account. In spite of all of their illogical and fantastic elements, fight scenes often maintain a certain sense of verisimilitude—a sort of "kabuki logic" accepted by what were (and still are) very critical audiences.

The odd thing, however, is that Shizuka, during much of the rest of the play, is depicted as the perfect courtesan lover, whose desire to follow Yoshitsune into danger is so strong, she must be tied to a tree to keep her from following him. Her grief at being parted from him elicits fits of weeping in the most piteous fashion, and yet, armed with first a naginata, and then a sword and a mission, she proves herself more than a match for both an oversized retainer and a magical fox.

The Vengeful Witch

Yamamba are mountain witches, and they have long held a place in Japanese folklore. The kabuki version of *Komachi Yamamba* is based on a puppet play by Chikamatsu Monzaemon, which premiered in 1712 and was adapted to kabuki in 1795 (Aragoro, n.d.: 1).

As usual in puppet plays and kabuki, the plot is complicated and contains a lot of not-very-logical twists. A courtesan named Yaegiri Oginoya appears at the home of Princess Omodaka. She can hear music from inside that was written by her husband, whom she is seeking. Yaegiri convinces the inhabitants that she is a fortuneteller, and they invite her inside to take part in the entertainment that is already underway. Once inside she finds her husband, disguised as a tobacco seller, taking part in the merriment. Yaegiri's husband was supposedly engaged in a vendetta against the man who murdered his father, and she is angry that she finds him here instead. When he learns that the murderer has already been dispatched, he commits suicide out of remorse, vowing his spirit will enter his wife and give her great power (Aragoro, n.d.: 2). At that point, a group of enemies comes to abduct the princess. Her brave lady-in-waiting, Shiragiku, draws her short sword and leaps to her defense. She manages to hold off several spear-wielding assailants, chasing them off the stage. Yaegiri, now thoroughly transformed by her husband's spirit into Yamamba, holds off the remaining attackers as much by magic as by martial prowess. At the end of the scene, Yamamba steps onto the back of one of the attackers, hair askew, magical power almost shooting out of her fingertips. To say that this scene is theatrically satisfying is a vast understatement. In this play, the female characters are not only clearly the righteous ones, but they have the courage and martial skill to triumph over their male adversaries, in spite of being outnumbered.

Female Loyalty

Finally, we turn to a quintessential play of female loyalty and vengeance, *Mirror Mountain: A Women's Treasury of Loyalty (Kagamiyama)*, premiering in 1782. Like its male counterpart, *The Treasury of Loyal Retainers*, *Mirror Mountain* is also a puppet play that was adopted into kabuki the following year. It was written by Yo Yotai, a physician who had regular access to samurai homes. The ostensible reason for writing *Mirror Mountain* was to specifically appeal to female audiences, particularly of the samurai class. *Mirror Mountain* was often performed in the spring of the year, when samurai women traveled to the cities for several days on their annual visits to their homes (Brandon & Leiter, 2002: 175). Given this highly critical audience, the depiction of life in a high-ranking lord's home and the behavior of the women employed there must have been quite convincing. In fact, the plot of the play was taken from several true incidents, including one involving the powerful Maeda clan, in which a maidservant of the samurai class took revenge for an act of humiliation endured by her mistress in 1724 (Brandon & Leiter, 2002: 174). There are fight scenes by female characters throughout the play. Interestingly, the major evil character, Lady Iwafuji, and her maidservants are actually played by male style actors.

At the beginning of the play, Lady Iwafuji, a bad-tempered lady-in-waiting to a princess of a powerful clan, challenges another lady, Onoe, to a fencing match. Onoe happens to be from the merchant class, and, as a result, never learned to fight. As she is being taunted by Iwafuji in the presence of the mistress, her servant, Ohatsu, appears. Ohatsu, though a low-ranking person in the household, is indeed from a samurai family and has been trained to fight. She avers that Onoe actually trained her, and offers to take part in the match in her place. Ohatsu, who turns out to be very skilful, bests Iwafuji in the match, having gotten so involved she has forgotten her lowly place as well as the fact that there may be repercussions for Onoe as she wins the fencing bout, injuring Iwafuji's hand in the process.

Iwafuji, enraged, takes vengeance on the gentle Onoe by stealing a block of precious incense wood the mistress had given her for safekeeping, replacing it with a slipper. Iwafuji then accuses Onoe of the theft, punishing her by beating her about the head with the slipper. Being publicly beaten in the face with an article of footwear, let alone unjustly, is too great an insult for Onoe to bear. She feels she has no choice but to return to her rooms and commit suicide. Ohatsu discovers her dying mistress and swears vengeance against Iwafuji, which she manages to do in another spectacular stage fighting scene, characterized by graceful onnagata movement. At one point, Ohatsu manages to wound Iwafuji in the shoulder, but there is no clear resolution to the fight. Eventually, Ohatsu lures Iwafuji close by feigning unconsciousness. When she draws near, Ohatsu stabs Iwafuji with the knife Onoe used to kill herself. She then takes the same slipper used to beat her mistress and beats Iwafuji's body with it, in payment of the insult that resulted in her mistress' death. Though Ohatsu makes preparations to follow Onoe in death, she is prevented from doing so and is hailed as a hero for destroying the evil Iwafuji. As a young samurai retainer, Motome, tells her:

> Iwafuji was an evil woman who was trying to destroy the clan. Ohatsu, you are a model of loyalty in killing Iwafuji to avenge the death of your mistress …
> – Brandon & Leiter, 2002: 212

The characters in the play use wooden practice swords for their fencing matches. There may be several reasons for this, one being theatrical necessity, as naginata, a more common weapon among women, are more difficult to manipulate onstage. Samurai women trained with a variety of weapons, including bows, short swords, knives, and even spears. Using wooden swords for the fencing scene was probably not that far removed from reality, or the female samurai audience would have reacted accordingly.

Mirror Mountain has not been as popular as its male-oriented counterpart, *The Treasury of Loyal Retainers* (which also includes an onnagata stage fighting scene, mentioned in the beginning of this paper), but it is still performed with some regularity. When I was observing classes at the National Theater of Japan in 1992, the acting teacher for female style, a retired onnagata, had earned acclaim in the 1950s for his portrayal of Ohatsu. I saw *Mirror Mountain* performed by an amateur kabuki troupe, and the stage fighting scenes were disappointingly shortened, but they were still good enough to contribute to a compelling theater experience. Created at a time when samurai were the de facto ruling class of the country, *Mirror Mountain* literally holds up a mirror to the experience of samurai women during the mid-Edo period.

Conclusion

This small set of examples shows that female characters, though not as belligerent as their male counterparts, were no strangers to engaging in fights in kabuki plays. Ohatsu is particularly arresting as she pants with excitement and needs to be calmed down from going further to injure Iwafuji than a simple tap on the wrist during the practice match. Shizuka exhibits a certain ferocity as she interrogates the false Tadanobu for the sake of her beloved. The largely female (and samurai) audiences for *Mirror Mountain* and other plays featuring martial female characters show that these role types were considered closer to the depiction of Edo period life than not, and the writings of Ayame and other onnagata emphasize the need for maintaining the illusion of realism for their audiences. The relatively normal appearance of fighting women roles in the context of the plays underscores the idea that martial arts training for women in certain classes of Japanese Edo period society was generally accepted. As I pursue my own training, I can look back on these women as distant forebears, even as the characters they admired continue to be brought to life by the fighting woman warriors of kabuki.

* **Note:** An earlier version of this chapter was given at the Performance Studies International conference held in Copenhagen, Denmark, in August, 2008.

Acknowledgments

The author wishes to thank the following people for their valuable assistance in preparing this article: Helen Moss, Oana Garcia, Emily Gordon, Chuck Gordon, and Mariano Garcia.

Bibliography

Aragoro, S. (n.d.). Yaegiri. www.kabuki21.com/yaegiri_kurawa_banashi.php (downloaded 7/8/08).

Brandon, J. and Leiter, S. (Eds.) (2002). *Kabuki plays on stage, Vol. 2: Villainy and vengeance 1773–1799*. Honolulu: University of Hawaii Press.

Dunne, C. and Torigoe, B. (Eds. and Trans.) (1969). *The actors' analects*. NY:

Columbia University Press.

Edgerton, R. (2000). *Warrior women: The amazons of Dahomey and the nature of war.* Boulder: Westview Press.

Fujita, M. and Shaprio, M. (Eds.) (2006). *Transvestism and the onnagata traditions in Shakespeare and kabuki.* Folkston: Global Oriental Ltd.

Hoppe, S. (1998). *Sharp spear, crystal mirror: Martial arts in women's lives.* Rochester, VT: Park Street Press.

Jones, D. (1997). *Women warriors: A history.* London: Brassey's.

Jones, S. (Tr.) (1993). *Yoshitsune and the thousand cherry trees.* NY: Columbia University Press.

Kabuki-za Theatre (1992). *Kabuki August 1992 program.* Tokyo: The Japan Times Ltd.

Keene, D. (Tr.) (1971). *Chushingura: The treasury of loyal retainers.* NY: Columbia University Press.

Kominz, L. (1997). *The stars who created kabuki: Their lives, loves and legacy.* Tokyo: Kodansha International.

Leiter, S. (2006). Female-role specialization in kabuki: How real is real? Transvestism and the onnagata traditions in Shakespeare and kabuki. Folkston: Global Oriental Ltd. pp. 70–81.

Matsubane Geino Productions (1992). *Kodomo kabuki kagamiyama kokyo no nishikie* (program). Tokyo: Mitsubane Geino.

Mezur, K. (2005). *Beautiful boys, outlaw bodies: Devising kabuki female-likeness.* NY: Palgrave MacMillan.

Pronko, L. (1971). Learning kabuki: the training program of the National Theatre of Japan. *Educational Theatre Journal,* 23(4): 409–430.

Sato, H. (1995). *Legends of the samurai.* Woodstock, NY: Overlook Press.

· 10 ·

Learning India's Martial Art of Kalarippayattu: Unsettled Ecologies of Gender, Class, Culture, and Ethnicity

by Sara K. Schneider, Ph.D.

Illustration courtesy of www.dreamstime.com

Introduction

The focus of the chapter is a cross-cultural, cross-gender guru-student relationship in *kalarippayattu*, a South Indian indigenous martial art. In it, I argue that both learning and the teacher-student relationship are inevitably colored by learner's and teacher's expectations and beliefs around appropriate gender, culture, and class behavior. The very media of teaching in this psychophysical form—attention; talk and silence; gesture, touch, and stillness—also draw in contrasting cultural frames.

Centering on the significance of two vignettes that took place in 2002 surrounding my fieldwork and participant-observation in Calicut, Kerala, India, this chapter surfaces both the gaps and the gains in undertaking study in another cultural setting, as well as the longing and the frustrations inherent in fieldwork. A specific ethnographic example underscores the complex ecologies of learning, where ostensible subject matter intersects with the teacher-student relationship and with the intricacies of gender, class, culture, and ethnicity.

The data come from fieldwork notes, videotapes, and photographs I took during two months of fieldwork in India during the period of May–September 2002, as well as from interviews I conducted with the kalarippayattu *gurukkal* (teacher/master) T. Sudhakaran, his teenage daughter and student, Archana, and groups of his school-aged male and female students. Such a recounting of the complexities of cross-cultural, embodied learning and teaching bridges the literatures on the teacher-student relationship, international education, and the anthropology of the body. It also asserts the centrality of embodiment in both international and American contexts of teaching and learning (Classen, 1993; Cooks & LeBesco, 2006; Freedman & Holmes, 2003; Geurts, 2002; Lave, 1977; Light, 2001; Ness, 1992).

With roots going back at least to the twelfth century, kalarippayattu is traditionally practiced by the Nayar caste, though members of other groups in South India have also taken it up. In Malayalam, the language of Kerala, its name means exercises (*payattu*) performed in a practice space (*kalari*). Revived in the 1920s as part of Kerala's resistance to British colonial rule, kalarippayattu is closely associated with Malayali images of manhood (Zarrilli, 2000). Boys I interviewed in Sudhakaran's C.V.N. Kalari in Calicut associated the practice with "becoming strong and healthy," with excellence in sports, and with the improvement of concentration (10 C.V.N. Kalari male school-age students, personal communication, September 2002). For those associating martial arts with upright postures acting as grounding for sharp, angular strikes by the limbs, a first view of kalaripayyattu can be startling. Its deep and wide preparatory squats, animal-inspired postures, and weapons combat feathered with spectacular leaps and turns all offer a stylistically contrasting image to many Westerners of the Eastern martial arts with which they may be more familiar.

The complexities of the experience stemmed in part from my entering into, belonging to (to some degree), and leaving a martial arts learning community as a person embodying the ambiguities of both high and low statuses. On the one hand, I was an upper-middle-class Western scholar, frequently treated (as are Euro-Americans and well-educated people generally) with what felt like exaggerated deference as being of equal or higher status to many Indians in this profoundly hierarchical society (Osella & Osella, 1998). There were also active lower-status valences attached to me, as, after all, I was a single, childless woman of childbearing age in a culture that sees wife and mother as primary roles for women. I was electing to study a martial art that, though it attracts young girls to its study, has relatively few adult female practitioners, much less girls practicing after puberty. Even though I continued to ask many questions in the course of and after practice lessons, in making the transition from verbally and visually engaged scholar to embodied student, I suffered a palpable change in status, one that perplexed me at the time and that later revealed larger insights about the roles of touch and talk in an embodied subject of learning.

1) Morning drill in one of many of the crouches of kalarippayattu. **2)** Master Sudhakaran mirroring his youngest student's movements in a kalari in Calicut, Kerala, India.

The Role of the Guru in the Transmission of Knowledge in Kalarippayattu

In American English, the term "guru" is as readily bandied about as are commercial terms like "Kleenex," "Xerox," and "Google." For Westerners, the term can refer to a leading practitioner or tastemaker, even if the person doesn't directly teach, or it may be invoked disparagingly to designate a currently popular expert, one the radio stations go to for a sound bite. By contrast, in India, the figure of the guru is defined through relationship and sacred responsibility. Originally, the guru was a teacher of the holy Vedic texts, and he (for it certainly was a he) had to be a member of India's highest caste, a Brahman; the term guru could also apply to a teacher of the traditional arts and crafts (Kale, 1970). The guru's disciples, who could be drawn from any part of Indian society, spent their adolescence living with his family and receiving the tradition orally. The guru's teaching was priestly, made essentially as a gift to his students; it was only rewarded at the end of their years together by whatever each student chose to give him.

With the rise of the devotional *bhakti* movement in Hinduism, and its development through the Indian medieval period, as well as the ascendancy of Buddhism and Jainism in India, the notion of the guru as an inspirational figure—even if not particularly learned figure—began to emerge. Rather than expecting that he would prove himself by his knowledge, the guru's students would invest him with faith. A form of guru worship, or *guru yoga*, dictated that the disciple submit himself without question, as a form of self-surrender or self-transcendence, to whatever request the guru might make.

3) Part of choreographed sequence performed across the length of the kalari. **4)** Focused practice. **5)** The oldest girls practicing in this kalari, other than the guru's 14-year-old daughter.

It is perhaps this unquestioning submission embedded in the term guru that raises many Westerners' hackles; the uncritical acceptance of someone as an expert may reek of cultism. No less suspicious from this perspective is that person who would accept another's seemingly blind obedience. Even in India, the unquestioning view of the guru eroded to a certain degree with British colonial rule, as Indians experienced a very different kind of teacher, one caught up in a wide bureaucratic net whose ultimate authority was the British government.

When I went to India, I was already somewhat familiar with the figure of the guru from two years of yoga study. In American *ashrams* (religious retreat) I had seen disciples place in their gurus' hands full authority to make such weighty decisions as selecting a suitable marriage partner for them. As is common practice in kalarippayattu, my teacher's students called him by the plural *gurukkal*, indicating his representation and incarnation of a long line of teachers in his tradition in which he stood as that line's culmination and apex (Zarrilli, 2000, p. 301).

While I spent some time observing martial arts practice at the southern kalari with which the Western expert on the form, Dr. Phillip B. Zarrilli, is best associated, I wanted to undertake study in a traditional village setting and traveled up the coast to spend the most time at a kalari in the north of Kerala. During my first trip to Calicut (Kozhikode), Kerala's third-largest city, I photographed and videotaped Sudhakaran's work with his students; observed the young people in training and practice; and sat in on rehearsals and demonstrations of the kalarippayattu performance troupe, which did shows for tourists staying at the higher-end hotels. Struck by this well-educated, well-traveled guru's use of corporal teaching methods, in May 2002, I wrote in my field notes: "Gurukkal teaches by a variety of methods. One of the more interesting … is by rapping the students with a stick, sometimes hard. He believes that this is the way to help children learn/remember. He does use their names when correcting them."

As threat of nuclear war with Pakistan arose in June 2002, foreigners were evacuated from South India. When in August I returned to Kerala, I knew that studying under Sudhakaran would mean altering my relationship to him. I had already adopted two relatively powerful roles with him, as researcher and as possible stage director, since I was interested in creating a more-elaborate production showcasing the performance strengths of the martial art for national and international audiences. To these roles I was adding that of student or, as Sudhakaran put it, disciple, and adopting the mores of his kalari. In addition, in order to make it to early morning and evening practice, I would be moving from a hotel in the town of Calicut out to the town's outskirts, where the kalari was located, and would be renting a room from Sudhakaran's immediate neighbors on the family compound, his brother and sister-in-law.

After Sudhakaran accepted me as his student in September, I struggled mightily with giving up my collegial status with him. I noticed that I resisted, with all my American commitment to egalitarianism, calling him by the honorific gurukkal, which was now more appropriate than for me to continue to use his given name; I associated the term with an unquestioning adoration that, again as an American, I balked at. As I somewhat agitatedly wrote in my field notes,

> If he were fully a guru to me—if I accepted this relation as the outright one—then I would want his approval utterly. I would want to know what I can be doing better as a person. But there's a part of me that wants to remain colleagues on a very buddy-buddy basis (doesn't want to move to student status), wants to hold his opinion in contempt, or to regard what he's about as somehow more "primitive" than what I'm about! [Yet what makes] ass-kissing primitive???

Contemporary ethnographers such as Behar (1996) have written sensitively about the ethical, relational, and procedural complexities of their fieldwork experiences. Behind their prefatory explications of how they built rapport with their subjects, dealt with unexpected relational developments, and made freighted ethical and practical choices in the course of collecting data and writing up their studies, lies their evident desire to help their audiences understand the methodology and the filters that have shaped their data. As readers, we are to understand that what they "got" was largely what they, as themselves unmistakably enculturated researchers, were able to "get"—to see, to hear, to understand. There is no guarantee that what ethnographers observe from the outside is what the data means in its own context; in part, the ethnographer's hope is that, by revealing her biases, predispositions, and history, the reader herself will be able to see through some of the necessarily partial interpretations to a clearer view of the data itself.

In sharing this ethnographic reflection, I hope to surface the role of a highly specific body—white, Western, female, unattached to husband or child—in a cross-cultural learning situation. The following two vignettes, which bookended my time in the C.V.N. Kalari, Calicut, demonstrate both my attraction to the teaching and learning world presented as well as my recognition of its limitations.

The gurukkal offering verbal corrections in mid-sequence.

When and What the Teacher Teaches Through Touch
~ Two Bookending Vignettes ~

Vignette 1: The Teacher's Blessing

Immediately after entering the kalari, the teacher, bare to the waist, begins to pray at each of the platforms placed around the periphery of the small, moist red clay-floored and clay-walled structure. His contemplative clockwise circuit reminds me of the Catholic stations of the cross, with time spent in apparent prayer or reflection at a series of spatially demarcated centers, each with one or more of the Hindu deities associated with the martial art. As they continue in their warm-ups in the thatched kalari, his six- to twelve-year-old students watch him with quiet peripheral awareness, mindful not to disturb him in his spiritual preparation for the morning's practice.

But just as soon as he completes his circuit of the platforms, the youngest students throng around him. As each student rapidly touches his fingers lightly to his teacher's feet and then to his own heart, and reiterates the gesture, the guru drops his hand to the crown of the student's head and carries it first to his own heart, then to the top of his head.

This customary blessing of each student, however, ends not with this gestural and energetic connection between the hearts and heads of teacher and student, via the guru's feet, but with a final gesture of the guru's hand. For, from the top of his student's and then his own head, the guru's hand carries up into space, as if to connect both the disciple's vulnerability and need to be blessed, and the guru's power to confer that blessing, with a greater source of power and learning that embraces them both.

As a yoga teacher and a university professor, this coda to the gesture of blessing touches me to the core. In it, I see the submission of both guru and *sisya*, or disciple, to a larger tradition that embraces them both. I experience with an unprecedented depth the honor of being a teacher—the humility and respect of the student, the love and faith of the teacher, but the submission of both within the gifts of knowledge and understanding for which both strive.

Vignette 2: The Withheld Hand

Some months later, I prepare to leave the C.V.N. Kalari, my guru, and the home of my hosts, my guru's brother and sister-in-law. I expect the goodbye to recall the simplicity and purity of the teacher's blessing that introduced me to the practice. Instead, real and perceived cultural and financial differentials of power dominate the scene.

My teacher instructs me to wind on, over my practice T-shirt, the red, white, and black *katcha*, a costume wrapped around the waist and through the legs for kalarippayattu demonstrations; his wife, Anitha, helps me. Sudhakaran doubtless knows I am still years of practice away from being qualified to take part in such a demonstration. Yet I know from other experiences, both with him and elsewhere during my fieldwork in India, that Westerners with sustained interest in Indian cultural practices can be ambushed into surprise photo sessions whose products can add cachet to a local institution. Photos of a Westerner in the C.V.N. Kalari can serve the kalari's, as well as the Kerala Tourism Commission's, long-range interests of showing that white Euro-Americans, as much as locals, find its training worthy.

Feeling uncomfortably objectified, I try to manage the photo taking so as to yield photos that I might be able to use as learning references. I naively ask the guru to pose with me as if he were correcting my postures—something that clearly still needs doing. He pauses for a moment, then, quite tentatively, allows his hands to alight on my shoulders, in a fashion both uncharacteristic of any other training correction I have ever seen—and entirely ineffectual as a correction for the posture I am doing.

1) Floor work to increase flexibility. **2)** Older students practicing leg exercises.

Suddenly, what has been slowly brewing in me over the training period comes to full consciousness: I recognize that he has not corrected a posture once by hand: that, by distinction with my male American counterpart, William, who trained for weeks beside me at the kalari, as a woman I have received what could be considered the illusion of training, for Sudhakaran has taught me largely through demonstration and discussion. Customarily, however, kalarippayattu is taught through verbal commands in Malayalam, rapid raps of the training stick on students' rumps or arms, and occasional hands-on adjustments, as are done in some forms of yoga. As a yoga student, in coming to India, I had been expecting hands-on corrections; my experience two years earlier of studying dance in Hindu Bali had instilled similar expectations. Indeed, I had gone to Indonesia to experience what dance training would be like when the student was like clay in a sculptor's hands; I'd hoped to contrast this learning experience with the far more verbal and modeling basis of teaching in ballet, the dance form in which I had grown up.

I suddenly flash back to a topic Sudhakaran had brought up, seemingly out of the blue, shortly after having accepted me as a student (Sudhakaran, personal communication, 2002). He had begun talking about gender relations in India as compared with in the United States and Europe. It is a fact, he said, that men and women are different. I wrote later that day, "I'm not clear what he thinks those differences are. But I am surprised that he explains to me a little more that when men touch women here, it is always sexual; even if a man and woman were to talk with each other a few times in public, people [would] think something is going on." His speech had truly confused me: why had the topic even come up? Was there some subtext? Was he trying to keep some feeling for me at bay? Was he just trying to make sure I didn't touch him, as would be my custom in my own country and my own instinct? Now I realize he was explaining to me why William would receive a very different form of training than would I.

Already studying at the C.V.N. Kalari when I arrived, William was at once my companion and a thorn in my side. He was a fellow American with whom I could share cultural observations and travails during the training. On one hand, I was glad for his presence, as he helped to deflect the attention I would get as a single, white woman traveling alone, yet I also noticed the explosion of feelings that were very close to sibling-like rivalries with him: I was continually astonished by how much credence Sudhakaran seemed to grant William, who always seemed a bit of a hapless fellow to me, asking him, for example, whether he thought my digital camera of high quality.

At the same time as the shock of the realization of the gender-specific ground of my learning experience fills me, the photo shoot itself skyrockets in importance to me. I realize it may stand as the finest, though most unconventional, training I have received while in Calicut—here, as I silently adjust my own poses, my teacher waits silently, the corrective touch I have been craving supplanted by his critical gaze and his silence till I get it right enough. I try to self-correct, to distill the essence of each movement into a single pose that can capture the spirit of the full one. His saying nothing means my efforts are still "cold"; a slight change in his energy might mean I am "getting warmer."

The scene throws into relief the replacement of an impossible touch in this cross-gender training environment, as well as the remaining class basis of the interaction between this research subject and fieldworker, guru and student, and South Indian male teacher belonging to the historic warrior caste and a female learner from a purportedly classless American society. I had been so profoundly moved by the submission of both guru and disciple in the act of conferring the blessing that I would minimize any difficulties I would later have in accepting my role in the drama.

Experiencing an Other Experiencing Me as Other

The title of Caryl Churchill's 1968 play tells the story of this, as many cultural encounters: it was, in a sense, *The Marriage of Toby's Idea of Angela and Toby's Idea of Angela's Idea of Toby*. As an American somatic anthropologist, I was both open to examining my experience in a new culture and horrified to have entered into this hierarchical society with a specific and complicated social position assigned to me.

As may have been evident to the reader for some time, I came to the encounter with my own ethnocentrism quite intact. Primary of course was my very American belief in egalitarianism, with white people and people of color, women and men, all treated as being of equivalent worth. Thus, the projection of the two sides of the ethnic and gender pedestal onto which I was being placed was enormously disquieting.

Enacting "Toby's idea of Angela," I had at least three warring desires. One, as previously mentioned, was to retain my collegial relationship with Sudhakaran, rather than submit to him as guru. At one point in the training I found myself, perhaps laden with stories of corrupt gurus in the United States, obsessed with the worry (without any real foundation) that Sudhakaran may not have been the moral exemplar that I "needed" him to be.

Second, there was a certain attraction to Sudhakaran, a handsome, athletic man five years my senior; perhaps this was generated in part by the forbiddenness and charged quality of both physical and verbal contact. (There is of course a long history of female protégées projecting such feelings onto their male mentors.) I was also well aware, during the two months overall I spent in India, of being touch deprived, used as I was to greeting friends, fellow yoga practitioners, and occasionally students with a hug.

Finally, there was the much larger concern, common among anthropologists, about usurping a cultural practice and profiting by it without offering an appropriate share of the benefits with the people whose tradition it is. I struggled with this issue, especially as I was funding my own research there. Did I really want to be the sole exploiter, demanding that in a relatively short period of research Keralans yield up their techniques and secrets to me, only to have me go away and make something of them?

Moving to the side of "Toby's idea of Angela's idea of Toby," to the people with whom I worked in India, I believe I was many things—someone who was neither Hindu nor Muslim; a single, childless female traveling alone; a fair-skinned Euro-American. I felt oddly depersonalized as I was faced with identity categories with unaccustomed significances. Sudhakaran and his family had had little or no prior experience of Jews; those who were neither Hindu nor

Muslim were by default honorary Christians. In addition, as a woman in India, I was someone whose skin and shape had to be concealed in public; who—as Sudhakaran had tried to help me understand—could not be seen speaking alone with, or be touched by, a man without others assuming a sexual relationship in this publicly chaste society. I hoped to learn kalarippayattu in the snug, sleeveless yoga tops that I had brought along for practice in the hot weather, but they were immediately forbidden by the guru, and I was sent shopping for more modest T-shirts. There was no room for the collegial or friendly male-female touch to which I was quite accustomed in the United States, nor for the open, body-conscious female athleticism I was accustomed to in the yoga world of Chicago. Finally, as a Euro-American, I received in India a consistent projection as potential benefactor, whether financial or networking for Indians toward international career opportunities.

1) Older students practicing the short stick set sequence. **2)** Young students practicing with long staffs. **3)** Practicing under the teacher's watchful eyes. **4)** Students receiving the gurukkal's blessing before leaving practice.

Frequently, I felt as if I were being spoken to out of two contrary codes: one that would be used for honorary high-caste persons and one I associated with the disregard shown to native women in India, even in the relatively liberal state of Kerala. Neither projection was comfortable for me, and I less-than-half-jokingly strove with one of Sudhakaran's friends, Prasad, who seemed somewhat more comfortable with Western customs than was my guru, to get him to think of and treat me not as a white female, but as he might an Indian male! Letting alone its practicality, conceptually this appeared (naturally) ridiculous to him—though to me at the time it seemed a solution to the discomfort of being socially elevated, treated as an ongoing sexual threat, or ignored.[1]

---

[1] And, as someone born Jewish and traveling in the most literate part of India less than a year after September 11, 2001, I was shocked to hear the theory that Israeli and American Jews were responsible for the terrorist attacks on New York's World Trade Center towers, that they had warned all Jews who worked in the building ahead of time to evacuate so that none of them would perish, and that none had. I later learned this theory is widespread in many parts of the world, including among many Muslims in Asia and the Middle East, and that it may be considered a twenty-first-century instantiation of the nineteenth-century anti-Semitic document *The Protocols of the Elders of Zion*, which posited that a secret, powerful group of Jews was striving to manipulate world events to serve Jewish interests (Anti-Defamation League, 2003, pp. 6–7; Neuman, 2005).

Corporal Teaching in Kerala

In the language of Bourdieu and Shilling, the "professional body" is a kind of "physical capital," able to turn the physical cultivation of years into a form of communication and development of others (as cited in Light, 2001). Lave (1977) highlighted the inductive basis of apprenticeship learning, which applies readily to training in Asian martial arts in general and specifically to kalarippayattu, as students practice with others of their own age and level; more-experienced students participate in the training of the less advanced; and the guru serves as the ultimate exemplar, not just the arbiter, of practice. In the kalari in Trivandrum, in the south of Kerala, that I visited, as well as the C.V.N. Kalari in Calicut, students practice alongside peers working at their own age and expertise level, which were generally linked. Thus, all students who were at my level were loincloth-wearing boys half my size or young girls in shorts and T-shirts, giggling and peeking out at me from behind bushes.

In kalarippayattu, students are taught by rote repetition. They practice the movements as the guru calls them out and gives them physical corrections. Underlying meanings come with time. As Sudhakaran explained to me in an interview, young students are only given the spiritual context for what they are doing once the teacher feels they are ready (Sudhakaran, personal communication, September 2002). While he will give his youngest students the basic outline of the actions they are to perform as they circle the kalari in worship, he considers early religious training to be the parents' responsibility. Thus, he will not go into extravagant detail at first on the mental state they should cultivate as they pray before each of the deities around the kalari's periphery: telling a person too early in life to channel the power of the gods for his practice will only distract him, in this guru's view.

Using a stick in correcting a student.

A good deal of teaching in kalarippayattu is done through the guru's verbal articulation of the movements in the time they are to be performed and through his touch, which is frequently mediated by one of the yard-long bamboo sticks that are the student's first weapon. Sudhakaran would, for example, incline a squatting student's upper body farther forward by leaning the bamboo stick across his back. Trainers of adult students of kalarippayattu in the southern Kerala city of Trivandrum also use the stick as a guiding corrective. One teacher I observed used his stick to correct the turnout of a student's leg or the position of his lower back, hips, or chest. Sudhakaran told me that inferior teachers would notice their students' mistakes but elect not to correct them (Sudhakaran, personal communication, September 2002).

The corporal punishment of students was outlawed by India's Supreme Court only in 2000, and the prohibition has been only laxly enforced. Still, in 2002, with young students in Kerala, corporal punishment appeared to be a regular teaching and disciplinary strategy. I saw Sudhakaran swiftly rap a student who hadn't put into practice a previous correction or was failing to pay attention; the boys in his kalari characterized the use of the bamboo pole in the kalari as far less than what their schoolteachers used on their hands when they misbehaved in school (personal communication, September 2002). Nevertheless, Sudhakaran's daughter, Archana, told me that whenever Westerners, with their frequent horror of corporal punishment, came to the C.V.N. Kalari, her father toned down the frequency and intensity of his more-punishing corrections, so she believed I was being exposed to less physical correction than a Keralan might have been (personal communication, September 2002). Euro-Americans generally have significantly longer-lived prohibitions against the corporal punishment of students; New Jersey outlawed the practice in public schools as early as the 1860s, while much of continental Europe and many of the United States have banned it in recent decades.

Even customary verbal exhortations can be questioned by Westerners. During my time in Kerala, I visited the Kerala Kalamandalam in Cheruthuruthy, where boys are molded, both manually and technically, into performers of *kathakali*, the highly stylized dance-drama form that draws heavily on kalarippayattu (Zarrilli, 2000: 3). Kalamandalam master Ramadass related the story of teaching a Dutch student who questioned his instructional shouting when he made a mistake; he argued that, as he wasn't from Kerala, why should the teacher verbally abuse him in the Keralan fashion? This interaction, which Ramadass described as being profound for him, caused him to alter his teaching behavior around foreign students—though he continued to yell at native ones (Ramadass, personal communication, August 2002).

Young boys in particular can be subjected to quite serious corporal punishment. At the Kalamandalam, tales of abuse of students are legendary. Two teenage students told me the story of providing emotional and medicinal salve to younger boys who suffered welts on their bodies from a guru's beatings (Piyal & Gautam, personal communication, September 2002).

In physical disciplines performed to music, such as kathakali and classical Indian dance, the gurus often have sticks handy for keeping time as the students practice. However, the sticks are obviously handy for more than beating time. I observed one kathakali teacher at the Kalamandalam go along a line of boys standing against the wall in his classroom, chiding and smacking each of them in turn. As I watched, he turned his focus on one, whacking him several times on the back of the head, while speaking caustically to him. Reminiscent of Hollywood films depicting boot camp training for the armed services, the boy of the moment would gaze stoically in front of him, never reacting openly, while the next boy in the lineup kept his own eyes also focused straight ahead and would appear unconcerned until the teacher began to speak to him.

Beatings can be both condoned and subject to some rebuke, though it's unclear how firmly it stands. Ramadass told me about being suspended after having been (perhaps falsely) accused of having injured students with beatings. He was reinstated but is cautious and reported never beating students again (Ramadass, personal communication, August 2002).

Even the pedagogical strategies that are not physically violent can be quite harsh emotionally. During the final kathakali examinations I saw, each student demonstrated twenty minutes' worth of material—a long time to be subjected to the judgment and close observation of two teachers, five classmates, and a Euro-American female visitor. Like kalaripayyattu students, kathakali students at the Kalamandalam are believed to learn from watching each other. During the examinations, if he saw the student making a mistake, the teacher, Krishna Kumar, would stop the dancing and ask first him, and then his classmates, what was wrong with his performance.

Overall, the examination room would be filled with the instructor's derisive laughter, ridicule, and negative reinforcement, both physical and verbal. Later, Ramadass told me that he never tells a student when he has actually done well (personal communication, August 2002). The student only learned the teacher's impression of him when his parents got his report card with a score and his class rank.

Conclusion

In the first vignette, which took place on my first day at Sudhakaran's C.V.N. Kalari, I was an observer, a witness to a customary Keralan scene of seeking and offering blessing and of demonstrating respect between guru and disciple as well as for the tradition and practice that embraced them. I saw touch and its evanescence as it was practiced and performed among those who belonged to it. I have no sense that anything was altered for my viewing, either in Sudhakaran's behavior toward his disciples, or in theirs toward him.

Many things had changed by the time of the second vignette, which closed my time at the C.V.N. Kalari. I was no longer a distanced videographer, photographer, and interviewer staying at the tourist hotel in the town. I was now a disciple of my research subject, rooming with his brother's family across the street. The qualities of my own gendered, ethnic body would alter his practice—how he would teach, what he would choose to correct, where he would take me in the practice. I had not made a transition out of a role whose valence in Keralan culture made me uncomfortable: I was still fair-skinned, Euro-American, female, single, and childless but of childbearing age. When I determined to get closer to the practice of kalarippayattu by way of my own kinesthetic intelligence—a mode I was recognizing as the readiest path for my own understanding —I paradoxically limited how close I would or could get to the understanding I sought.

So many ironies skeined the second vignette: the relative superficiality of the contact at the goodbye, even as we had had a greater length of time together, the willingness of the gurukkal to portray an incompetent practitioner as a performer of the art for marketing purposes. Perhaps the greatest of these ironies, and the moment that provided the greatest insight of my time in Kerala, took place as Sudhakaran silently waited to reinforce me with the snap of the camera until I had sufficiently corrected myself—wrong still, so long as his machine remained silent. When he half-compliantly touched me on the shoulders without actually correcting me, I saw the utter absence of the teaching touch that I hadn't realized I'd been missing. In some sense, I was like the youngest children who would make the circuit of the kalari in the outward manifestations of prayer without full understanding of what they were to do at each station; I was practicing my way into the form with diminished maturity. Unlike them, however, I might never advance, so long as I was attempting to learn within a relatively traditional kalari, informed by local social norms as it was.

Much has been made of cross-cultural differences in direct and indirect communication, as well as in the varied uses of speech and silence, in teaching and learning (see, for example, Radford, 2009; Stahl, 1994; Tincani & Crozier, 2007). So too has scholarly attention focused on cross-cultural differences in eye contact as they may impact teaching and learning (Chiang, 1994; Pitton, Warring, Frank, & Hunter, 1994). Historically, in Western cultures, the principal way in which touch has been discussed as a teaching strategy is of course in the role of corporal punishment in disciplining unruly pupils. More recently, authors mourn the loss of touch in the American classroom in the wake of political correctness, societal litigiousness, and concerns about students' emergent sexuality. They also emphasize the gendered, indeed sexual, presence of the teacher (Cooks & LeBesco, 2006; Freedman & Holmes, 2003; Johnson, 2006; Sapon-Shevin, 2009).

The author in katcha on last
day of study with her hosts, the
gurukkal's sister-in-law and niece.

Sapon-Shevin's (2009) treatment of the loss for students when touch is withheld provides a rare voice. Certainly, my own longing for teacherly touch —which magnified after I realized I hadn't had it—had many sources, only a limited number of which could be attributed to the specifically cultural clash I generated by coming into kalarippayattu training as an adult woman expecting the same training a man would have gotten, just as I had in dance and yoga training in the States or, to some extent, in Hindu Bali. Nevertheless, this example displays the power of corrective touch given—and withheld—and highlights the qualities of the peculiarly intercultural form of training in which a traditional practice rests within traditional values, even in a globalizing society.

Bibliography

Anti-Defamation League. (2003). *Unraveling anti-Semitic 9/11 conspiracy theories.* New York: Gorowitz Institute. Retrieved April 20, 2010, from www.adl.org/anti_semitism/9-11conspiracytheories.pdf

Behar, R. (1996). *The vulnerable observer: Anthropology that breaks your heart.* Boston: Beacon Press.

Chiang, L. (1994). *Beyond the language: Native Americans' nonverbal communication.* (ERIC Document Reproduction Service No. ED 368540). Retrieved from ERIC database.

Churchill, C. (1968). *The marriage of Toby's idea of Angela and Toby's idea of Angela's idea of Toby.* Unpublished play.

Classen, C. (1993). *Worlds of sense: Exploring the senses in history and across cultures.* New York: Routledge.

Cooks, L., and LeBesco, K. (2006). Introduction: The pedagogy of the teacher's body. *The Review of Education, Pedagogy, and Cultural Studies,* 28: 233–238.

Freedman, D., and Holmes, M. (Eds.) (2003). *The teacher's body: Embodiment, authority, and identity in the academy.* Albany: State University of New York Press.

Geurts, K. (2002). *Culture and the senses: Bodily ways of knowing in an African community.* Berkeley: University of California Press.

Johnson, T. (2006). Performing a/sexual teacher: Cartesian duality in education. *The Review of Education, Pedagogy, and Cultural Studies,* 28: 253–266.

Kale, P. (1970). The guru and the professional: The dilemma of the secondary school teacher in Poona, India. *Comparative Education Review,* 14(3): 371–376.

Lave, J. (1977). Cognitive consequences of traditional apprenticeship training in West Africa. *Anthropology and Education Quarterly*, 8(3): 177–180.

Light, R. (2001). *The body in the social world and the social world in the body: Applying Bourdieu's work to analyses of physical activity in schools*. Retrieved July 15, 2009, from http://www.aare.edu.au/01pap/lig01450.htm

Ness, S. (1992). *Body, movement, and culture: Kinesthetic and visual symbolism in a Philippine community*. Philadelphia: University of Pennsylvania Press.

Neuman, J. (2005, October 21). *History of the world, Part 2: Jewish conspiracy theory: The satire*. Slate. October 21. Retrieved April 20, 2010 from http://www.slate.com/id/2128525/

Osella, C., & Osella, F. (1998). Friendship and flirting: Micropolitics in Kerala, South India. *Journal of the Royal Anthropological Institute*, 4(2): 189–206.

Pitton, D., Warring, D., Frank, K., and Hunter, S. (1994). *Multicultural messages: Nonverbal behaviors in the classroom*. (ERIC Document Reproduction Service No. ED362519). Retrieved from ERIC database.

Radford, J. (2009, August). Word searches: On the use of verbal and non-verbal resources during classroom talk. *Clinical Linguistics and Phonetics*, 23(8): 598–610.

Sapon-Shevin, M. (2009). To touch and be touched: The missing discourse of bodies in education. In H. Shapiro (Ed.), *Education and hope in troubled times: Bold visions of change for our children's world* (168–183). New York: Routledge.

Stahl, R. (1994). *Using "think-time" and "wait-time" skillfully in the classroom* (May 1994 report). (ERIC Document Reproduction Service No. ED30885). Bloomington, IN: ERIC Clearinghouse for Social Studies/Social Science Education.

Tincani, M., and Crozier, S. (2007, September 25). Comparing brief and extended wait-time during small group instruction for children with challenging behavior. *Journal of Behavioral Education*, 16: 355–367. Retrieved from ERIC database.

Zarrilli, P. (2000). *When the body becomes all eyes: Paradigms and practices of power in kalarippayattu, A south Indian martial art*. Oxford: Oxford University Press.

· 11 ·

Why Women Need Sunzi's Book *The Art of War*

by Becky Sheetz-Runkle, B.A.

The Art of War copied on bamboo during the reign of Emperor Qianlong (r. 1735–1796). Collection at the University of California, Riverside.

The *Art of War* is the world-renowned military classic written by the Chinese philosopher-general and military strategist, Master Sun (Romanized in pinyin as Sunzi; in Wade-Giles as Sun Tzu), around 500 B.C. His work has had profound influence, first on Eastern military and business thinking, and more recently here in the West. The popularity of *The Art of War* continues to grow as managers and leaders apply its principles, using war as a metaphor to meet and overcome business challenges. A plethora of Sunzi books, seminars, and training tools continue to emerge. However, particularly in the West, Sunzi has been embraced primarily by men and ignored by women.

This disproportionate treatment is unfortunate, as Sunzi has a great deal to teach women all around the world. Of particular interest to today's women in business are the many ways to apply his timeless military lessons for business success—without sacrificing uniquely feminine leadership styles. This was the examination I undertook when I wrote *Sun Tzu for Women* (2011).

However, as a lifelong martial artist, I find Sunzi's application for the self-defense arts especially fascinating. The guidance he provides, and that women can apply to the martial arts of self-defense, is particularly and deeply instructive and rewarding. Since my first reading of Sunzi many years ago, he has helped me better define and execute a martial arts strategy that has proven successful for me. He can do the same for others—women and men—in the martial arts.

Sunzi and Me (and You)

My journey is not unlike those of many women in the martial arts. I've always been smaller and less strong than adversaries on the mat, but I've also been very tenacious and dedicated. Because my focus has been first and foremost self-defense, I've had to adapt my training over the years to focus on a paradigm that made the most sense based on my attributes and my limitations. I've worked within the confines of traditional martial arts (first karate, and today aikijutsu), but, seeking not to follow in the footsteps of men of old, in the spirit of the poet Matsuo Basho, I've been encouraged to instead seek what they sought. This concept of understanding and leveraging your best assets is essential Sunzi.

With the sage battlefield wisdom of Sunzi as a backdrop, what follows are the traits and characteristics that women martial artists in particular must hone to be effective when it matters most. Sunzi tells us much about how best to hone them, embody them, and harness them. Men, too, can gain much from this reading, as they can apply Sunzi's words to their training and martial development. It's also my hope that all instructors working with women and girls in self-defense arts will take something from this chapter that they can use to aid in the development of their students. Self-defense is serious business and it was the business of Sunzi.

Principles and Techniques

Precise technique is the second-most-important trait a woman in martial arts must have. The most important trait comes later. Technique is a precursor to it.

Sunzi called for his ideal general to be a brilliant tactician. He called for flawless technique. Superb technique is just as important for women in martial arts who want to be successful in combat as it was for troops on the battlefield. The following elements of Sunzi's battlefield science are particularly apropos to women in martial arts.

Timing

Martial artists are quite familiar with the concept of timing. All martial arts seek to develop their practitioners' timing. Attacking when the opponent is well prepared is less likely to be effective than timing the attack to land when he is not prepared. In a combat scenario, being too late with a viable response can make the difference between living and dying.

Sunzi teaches that opportunities must be seized when you're ready and when your opponent is not: *Invincibility lies in the defense; the possibility of victory in the attack. Defend yourself when the enemy's strength is abundant, and attack the enemy when it is inadequate.*

Timing means alertness to opportunities that are presented to you, as well as readiness to create them: *Thus, one who is adept at keeping the enemy on the move maintains deceitful appearances, according to which the enemy will act. He lures with something that the enemy is certain to take. By so doing he keeps the enemy on the move and then waits for the right moment to make a sudden ambush with picked troops.*

Timing is no more or less important for women in martial arts than it is for men. But the precise application of timing may very well vary. With a joint-locking martial art such as aikijujutsu, the locks are applied with some level of standardization across the many styles of jujitsu. While there are certainly variations, the fundamental wrist-locking techniques are applied similarly across aikijujutsu dojos.

When applied properly, these wrist locks are done with impeccable technique and an absence of strength. But combat is fluid, and if the technique doesn't come on precisely as planned, practitioners go into the default mode of adding a little (or a lot) of muscle to get the desired result. I can tell you from personal experience as a practitioner and an instructor that philosophy will only work if you're stronger than the person who's attacking you. Unless you can guarantee that you'll always be stronger than an adversary or adversaries, timing is especially important.

I have learned over the years the absolute criticality of timing. Methods of harnessing timing include disrupting the opponent or breaking his balance—the concept of *kuzushi*—with a quick blow to a vulnerable body target, known as an *atemi*.

Sequence 1

The attacker comes in to grab (1a). Before he gets set and completes a firm grab, Sheetz-Runkle, delivers a vertical punch to the solar plexus (1b). Timing is of the essence. At this point, an infinite number of follow-up techniques are available.

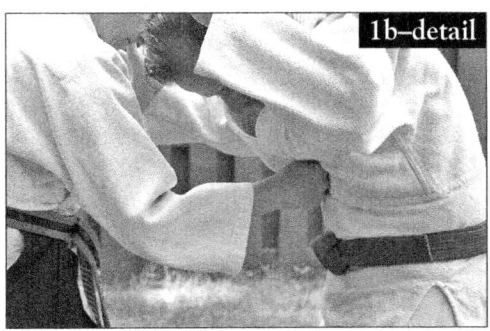

Reaction time is particularly critical to women and others of smaller stature. Once an attacker has laid his hands on you and has begun to apply pressure in the form of a bear hug, a choke, etc., the proverbial clock is ticking, and escape must happen quickly. A choke applied by an expert can rupture the trachea, quickly ending any ability for the victim to respond. Even chokes applied sloppily can cause panic and end a life well inside of a minute. For these reasons, it's important to react immediately. Reaction time is important for men and women, but because of the strength disparity, women are best served evading grabs before the attacker has fully set himself.

Sequence 2

The attacker comes in to grab (**2a**). As he attempts to do so, Sheetz-Runkle steps in with an elbow to his right jaw line, breaking his balance momentarily and distracting him (**2b**). She then delivers a knee to the torso (**2c**), then tightly pulls his head into her side as a leverage point. His right wrist is a second leverage point (**2d**). She then pivots and throws, with his neck and wrist as the basis (**2e**). This is a neck break if the head is fixed tightly as she pivots. Alternatively, he can be thrown to the ground and a kick can be delivered (**2f**).

"... swift as a running hare."
—Sunzi

Sequence 3

The attacker attempts a rear choke (**3a–b**). Before he's able to lock in the choke, Sheetz-Runkle deadweights and releases pressure around her neck, dropping his attacking arm down enough to escape the pressure on her neck and throat (**3c–d**). She then executes a thumb lock (**3e**), followed immediately with a nerve under the attacker's jawline (**3f**), dropping him to the ground (**3g**). She then drops a knee on his jaw (**3h**).

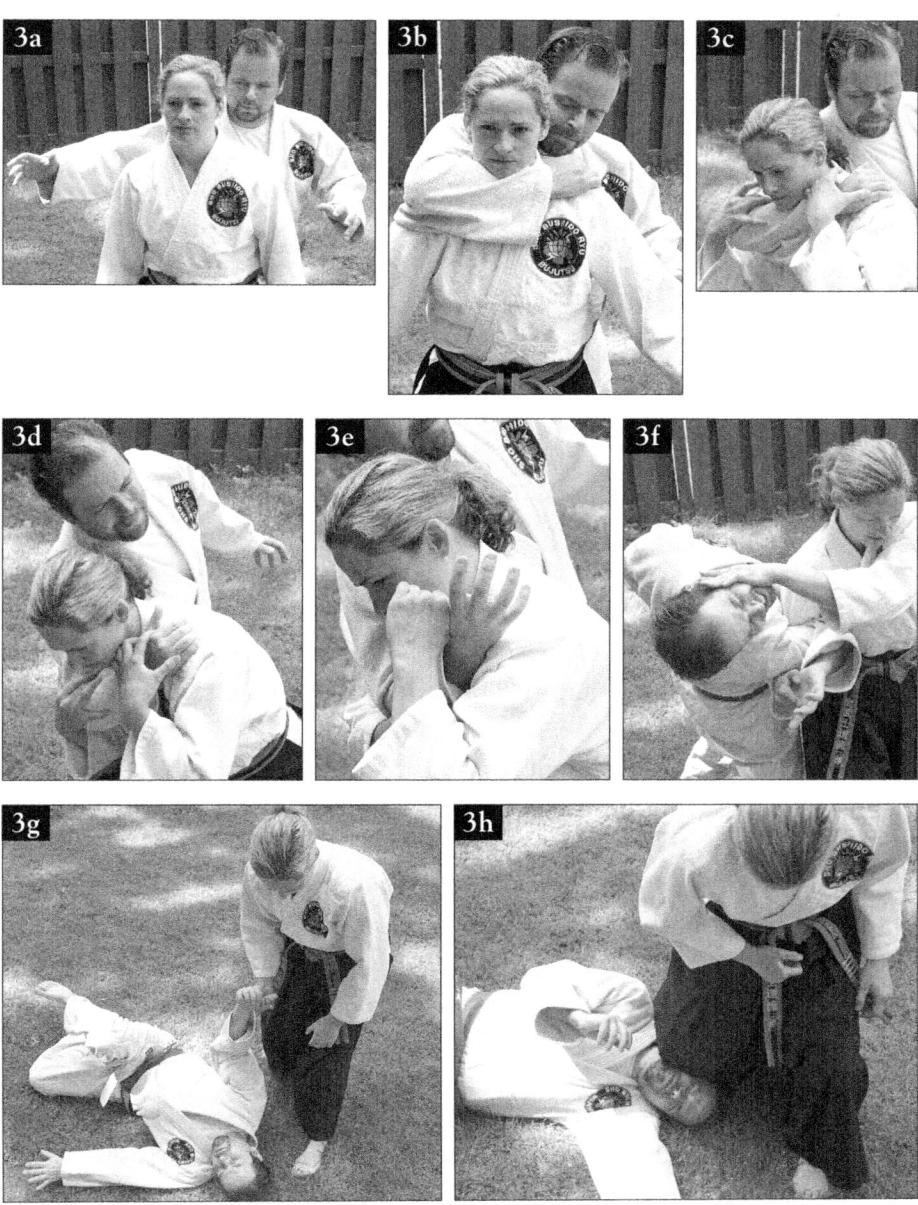

Create Opportunities and Seize Opportunities

The second technical element of Sunzi's battlefield science is seen in creating and seizing opportunities. While timing is critical here, taking advantage of these opportunities involves much more than the physical aspect. The ability to move in decisively and take advantage of an adversary's weakness involves a state of mind of being ready to achieve victory. Acting decisively and definitively greatly boosts your odds of meeting an unprepared adversary. Sunzi tells us to take advantage of every viable and authentic opportunity: *If the enemy leaves a door open, you must rush in. Seize the place the enemy values without making an appointment to battle with him. Be flexible and decide your line of action according to the situation on the enemy side.*

Sunzi is saying to launch your attack, or defense, at the most opportune time. The *dojo* applications are many when defending yourself against a sparring partner or in *randori* (freestyle practice). But on the street, there's no luxury of making mistakes and learning from them for the next practice. Sunzi says, once the opportunity has been created, *be swift as a running hare, and it will be too late for the enemy to oppose you.*

Opportunities created will provide no benefit if you're not prepared to seize them. The technical knowledge, as well as the mindset that must accompany it (which is discussed below), are necessary for reacting quickly, definitively, and successfully.

Prepare for Consequences

The Art of War is a very short book, but throughout it, Sunzi repeatedly calls for exhaustive preparation. The skilled general must be ready for any conceivable or inconceivable battlefield scenario, he advises. This mentality must also be adopted by martial artists. Preparation begins in the mind. For the martial artist this starts with the realization that we may very well be attacked, anywhere and at anytime. Moreover, the odds may be very much against us. For women in martial arts this comes with the added responsibility of training based on what an actual attack may look like. Altercations between two men, or between a man and a group of men, are often very different from those involving a woman as the victim or would-be victim.

A female practitioner must train with the understanding of the battlefield scenarios in which she may find herself. While this doesn't call for a different arsenal of self-defense than it does for a man, it does require the realization that the combat scenarios will likely be different. To be successful, preparation must match those realities.

Sequence 4

The attacker grabs (**4a–b**) and then attempts to slap or punch with his free hand (**4c**). Sheetz-Runkle steps in and blocks (**4c**), delivers a quick elbow strike (**4d**), and then traps his grabbing arm (**4e**). She then executes the jujitsu wrist locking/breaking technique of *nikkyo* (**4f–g**), followed by an armbar and wrist lock to immobilize him on the ground (**4h**).

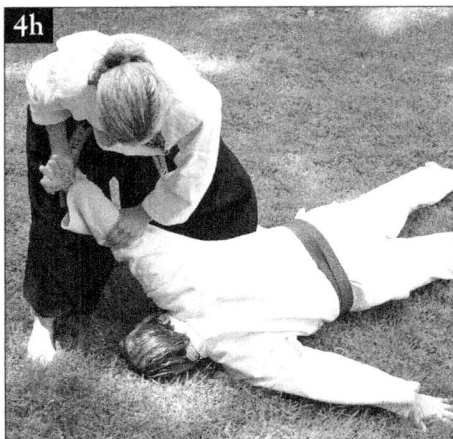

Of course, not everyone takes advantage of the opportunities presented. This ability to take advantage makes more than a small difference for Sunzi. Fear of consequences of taking advantage is often a major barrier. It's easy to second guess ourselves and ask, "What if the timing isn't right? What if I'll get hurt in the process? What if I fail?"

For Sunzi, these are questions that are to be answered as you prepare yourself for battle. Once you're ready to move in and seize the opportunity, the time for asking questions is over. Rush in through the open door.

Speed

Sunzi consistently emphasizes the importance of moving quickly to overtake an unprepared adversary: *Speed is the essence of war. Take advantage of the enemy's unpreparedness, make your way by unexpected routes, and attack him where he has taken no precautions.*

There is a great deal in those two sentences above. Speed, of course, is essential for all martial artists. But for women in particular, we absolutely have to be able to launch attacks and defenses quickly, or to be able to evade and launch a speedy retreat. Hesitation can be devastating. All things being equal, delayed responses for male counterparts aren't necessarily as deadly. Men are able to absorb more and heavier blows than women, and able to fight their way out with strength when necessary. It's my steadfast belief that women in martial arts should adapt a slight variation of Sunzi's belief: "Speed is the essence of self-defense."

Speed is the ability to apply impeccable timing, create and seize opportunities, and prepare for consequences. As Sunzi says, take advantage in unexpected ways, and when he's not ready. Distraction can play a role here. Rather than wait for an assailant to get a firm hold, place a weapon against you, or knock you to the ground, women should practice and apply a self-defense strategy of catching him off guard. For example, when his attention is fixed on harming you, ask him, "Do you really want to do this with all those people looking?" When he looks at the make-believe people, you launch your attack, take the gun, etc. This is both creating an opportunity and taking advantage of his momentary unpreparedness.

Sequence 5

This is an illustration of taking advantage of a very narrow window of opportunity. The attacker has pulled a knife, but hasn't yet thrust it forward (5a). Sheetz-Runkle closes the distance (5b), stepping offline of the knife and slightly parrying (5c). She then quickly delivers an eye jab (5d), followed by a come-along wrist grab (5e). The wrist can either be broken at this point (**5f–g**) or the attacker can be taken to the ground into a painful bargaining position (**5h–i**), where any number of opportunities avail themselves.

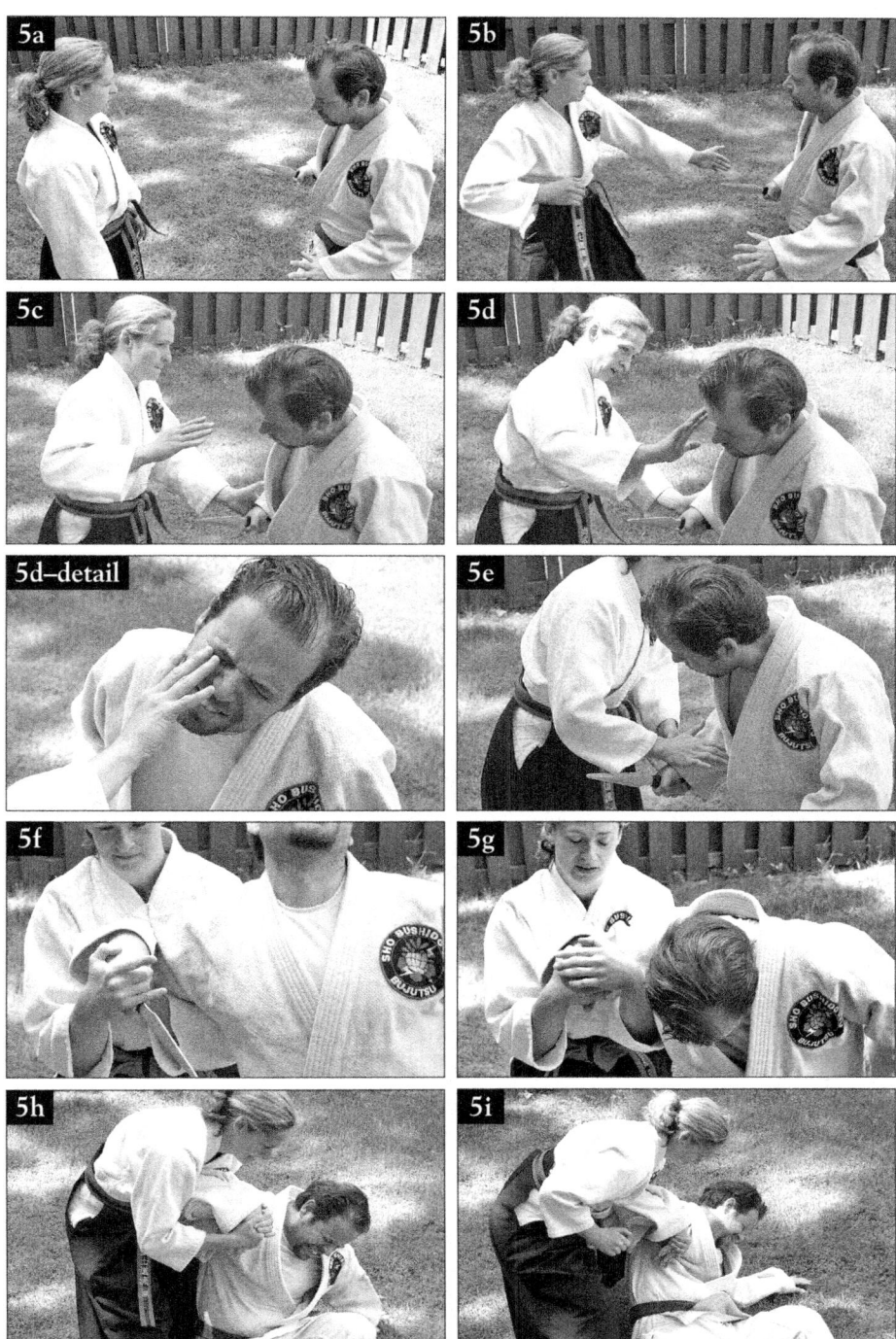

Perhaps all this talk about women's relative disadvantages in the martial arts is discouraging. However, it's not all negative. Sunzi encourages his general to turn disadvantages to advantages. Female martial artists have a distinct advantage when it comes to Sunzi's direction to *make your way by unexpected routes*. Foremost, the person who attacks you doesn't expect you to put up much of a defense. After all, cowards go after weakness, not strength.

As mentioned previously, women and men are attacked differently. So rapidly applying a defense will be unexpected and will help you to gain an advantage. In this way, you will allow your enemy to be ill prepared in his overconfidence. *All warfare is based on deception. Therefore, when able to attack, we must pretend to be unable; when employing our forces, we must seem inactive; when we are near, we must make the enemy believe we are far away; when far away, we must make him believe we are near.*

Then, after you have lured the enemy in by shaping perception, manipulating circumstances, or causing disorientation, be ready to launch your decisive attack: *That you are certain to take what you attack is because you attack a place the enemy does not or cannot protect.*

Spirit

Technique is the second-most-important self-defense trait for women in martial arts. Spirit is the single most important attribute. The most finely honed skill and precision means next to nothing without a strong fighting spirit. When I teach self-defense classes, the first thing I tell women is that I can teach them lots of tactics, but I can't teach them that their lives are worth fighting for. Self-defense class students are one thing. Serious martial artists are something else entirely. But sadly, in my years of training, I've seen a fair number of such women who didn't have the confidence necessary to defend themselves if they needed to. A shodan who had trained in multiple arts told me she didn't believe she could hit a man and hurt him. If I believed as she did, I'd never leave my house. I've seen this confidence crisis exhibited among even very high-ranking female practitioners. Sunzi agrees that spirit is requisite for victory.

For Sunzi, victory begins well before the battle is fought. The woman (or man) who hasn't cultivated the spirit of self-belief will be unable to carry out useful tactics. This is true on the mat, in a parking garage, in business, and everywhere else in life.

There's much more to directed force than physical factors, as Sunzi tells us: *Throw your soldiers into a position whence there is no escape, and they will choose death over desertion. For if prepared to die, how can the officers and men not exert their uttermost strength to fight? In a desperate situation, they fear nothing; when there is no way out, they stand firm. Deep in a hostile land they are bound together. If there is no help for it, they will fight hard.*

Martial artists who train for the modern battlefield will understand the importance of blending the idea of taking unexpected routes with developing the battlefield spirit necessary to win—or at least live to fight another day. Here's a martial arts example to illustrate this.

I met my martial arts mentor, Uche Anusionwu, while we were undergraduates at Temple University in Philadelphia. When we met, I had been training for several years, had a couple of black belts, and was proud of my achievements. Uche, however, had been training hard from a very young age and was putting *The Art of War* into practice. He created opportunities, moved in, disrupted, confused, and simulated destruction. My training to that point had more boundaries and more rules. I was completely overrun by Uche.

I tried to view these sessions as necessary to improving, but I often just ended up getting beaten up and demoralized. I was tempted to stop training with this person who was so proficient at beating me. After all, if I didn't train with him, I wouldn't be reminded of my glaring weaknesses. We all feel better about ourselves when we aren't immobilized on our posterior, literally or metaphorically. Or, I could continue, find out what I needed to do to even the odds, and grow. I chose option number two.

After working with Uche for several years, I noticed a marked improvement. I was more aggressive, less fearful, more confident in myself, and better able to execute. Had I not left my comfort zone, I wouldn't have made the achievements I made in the years since. Today, I'd still be following a formulaic, predictable paradigm that didn't prepare me for the realities of combat. While these days were tough and defeating in the short term, the impact they had on my abilities and my confidence is beyond measure.

This illustrates both the importance of preparation as well as the spirit required by Sunzi.

Unleash Energy

Sunzi emphasizes unleashing energy, a concept that will be familiar to many practitioners of Asian martial arts. This is the culmination of timing, seizing opportunities, creating opportunities, and speed. In times of battle, attacks should be let loose with ferocity, according to Sunzi: *An army of superior strength takes action like the bursting of pent-up waters into a chasm of a thousand fathoms deep. This is what the disposition of military strength means in actions of war.*

Preparation

Preparedness is intertwined with both technique and spirit. You can't have impeccable technique without a great deal of practice, nor can you have the spirit of victory required by Sunzi without a mind, body, and soul ready to win. In a self-defense situation, your life may well be contingent upon your readiness for what lies ahead. Sunzi writes that if you've trained well and honestly assessed yourself, your adversary, and the conditions of battle, and you're ready, you can handle any encounter you'll face. Preparation is a defining factor in the outcome: *He who is well prepared and lies in wait for an enemy who is not well prepared will win.*

While martial artists aren't concerned with actively lying in wait for enemies, our training and our mindset should be centered on scenarios that may be in our future. The first element of achieving a state of preparedness is necessarily excellence. Sunzi requires excellence and always being in a state of readiness. If you allow yourself to slip into complacency, your skills—and, importantly, your confidence—will atrophy. While you often can't control what happens to you, you can control how you respond. You alone can define how ready you are for the challenge. Your greatest battle may be tomorrow. You must ask yourself, Are you ready for it?

The second element is realistic training. For women in particular, self-defense training has to be grounded in realism. Not only must scenarios be realistic, but they must be high intensity, fast, and hard. Practicing prescribed defenses against prescribed attacks is not preparation for the modern battlefield. Preparation requires readiness for the worst-case scenario. You must come to grips with the idea that it can happen to you first; then train for it.

Sequence 6

Realism must include effective training against firearms. Here the attacker pulls a gun (**6a**). Sheetz-Runkle steps offline (**6b**), drives the gun overhead (**6c**), and uses that momentum (and the unexpected) to rotate the attacker's elbow (**6d–g**) so she can execute an armbar and take the gun (**6h–i**). This is a very effective armbar execution because it enables her to drop her body weight onto the elbow joint as she drives her energy to the ground. Even with the strongest of attackers, elbow joint versus body weight, the elbow loses.

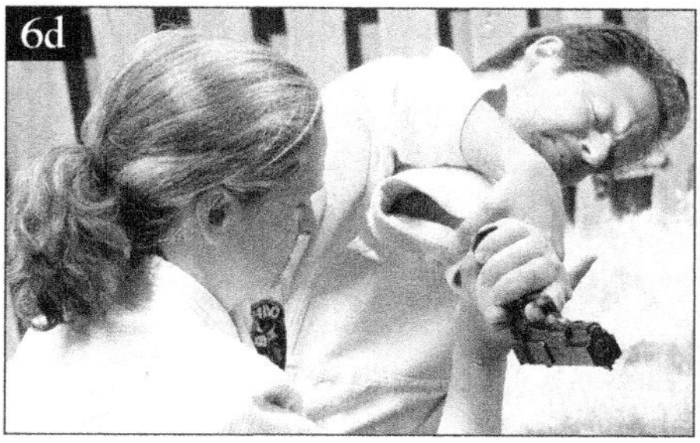

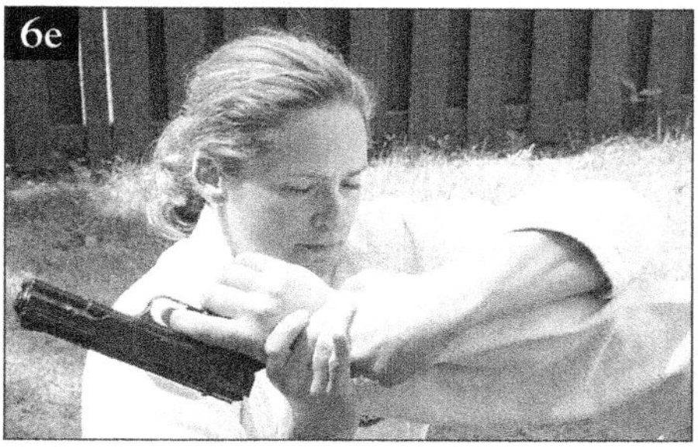

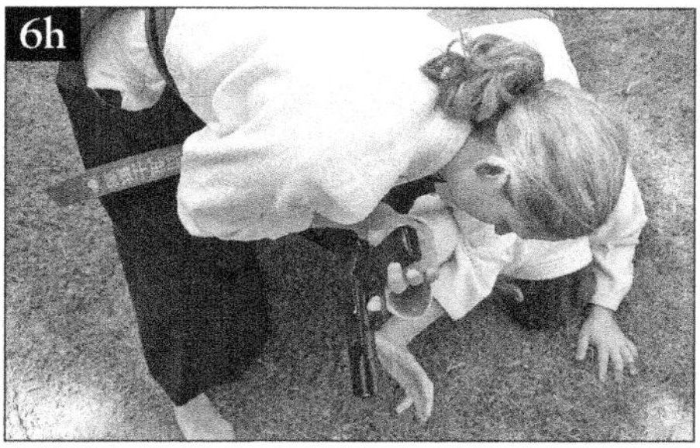

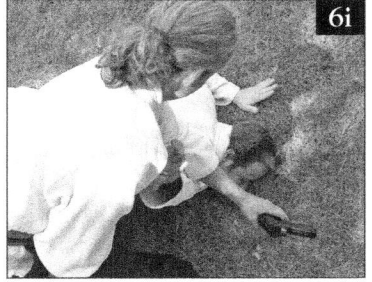

A statue of Sunzi—with *The Art of War* in his hand, and sword by his side—stands in a Chinese classical garden called Enchoen, located in Yurihama, Tottori, Japan.

Sunzi's advice is to be so well prepared for even the worst possible outcomes as to have already lived through them and overcome them. While Sunzi cautions that only those battles that can be won and will advance your cause should be fought, he realizes that not all situations you'll find yourself in will be optimal. You can turn worst-case scenarios to your advantage if you're prepared for them: *A wise general in his deliberations must consider both favorable and unfavorable factors. By taking into account the favorable factors, he makes his plan feasible; by taking into account the unfavorable, he may avoid disasters.*

A Mind Prepared for the Worst-Case Scenario

Here's a combat situation that illustrates what it's like to be ready for the worst-case scenario.

There have been fewer than one hundred female prisoners of war in U.S. history. *Brigadier General Rhonda Cornum, Ph.D., M.D.* On February 27, 1991, she was a flight surgeon aboard a Blackhawk searching for a downed F-16 pilot. Her helicopter was shot down. Cornum was among three soldiers who survived the crash. With two broken arms, a broken finger, torn knee ligaments, an eye glued shut with blood, a gunshot wound in the back, and other injuries, she climbed out from under the wreckage.

While being transported in Iraqi custody, Cornum then experienced what she sarcastically calls "the famous sexual assault." Badly injured, she was in no condition to fight back. She said her biggest concern wasn't rape, but that Sgt. Troy Dunlap, who was also taken captive, might find out and get killed trying to defend her. Cornum was held prisoner for eight days. Although she wasn't tortured, she never knew what the next day would hold. Cornum was mentally, physically, emotionally, and spiritually ready for the reality that she was going to war, could be taken prisoner, and could be mistreated. She saw her responsibility as staying alive until she was rescued.

Instead of being ensnared by fear, Cornum focused on what she could control. She gave Sgt. Dunlap rudimentary instructions for treating her broken arms. She focused on working to raise her pain threshold, initiating physical therapy, and beginning to heal, instead of focusing on the specter of interrogation and torture. She disciplined herself to keep track of the days and time. She and the two Iraqi women who were her keepers began teaching each other their languages.

Because she prepared herself for the risks she took, she was able to overcome her fear and survive her imprisonment. When she came home from Iraq, Cornum continued her distinguished military career. She is an example of Sunzi's direction to be always looking for ways of *snatching victory from defeat*. With resilience and indomitable spirit, she turned desperate disadvantages to a personal victory. Ready for the worst-case scenario, it didn't defeat her.

Finding Your Own Path

Women training in realistic, combat-oriented martial arts must always remember Matsuo Basho's sage advice: "Seek not to follow in the footsteps of men of old; seek what they sought." Your martial arts training will manifest itself differently than your male peers' for the reasons outlined in this chapter. But do not misunderstand me. This is not about being less effective or resigning yourself to your "weaknesses." Instead, your training should capitalize on your strengths and your attributes. You must be well tuned and uncompromisingly honest about what those are. You martial arts will be a picture of how well you know yourself, how well prepared and how carefully you've trained, and the strength of your fighting spirit.

References

Sheetz-Runkle, B. (2011). *Sun Tzu for women: The Art of War for winning in business*. Avon, MA: Adams Media.

Michaelson, G. and Michaelson, S. (2010). *Sun Tzu: The Art of War for managers: 50 strategic rules updated for today's business*. Avon, MA: Adams Media. All quotations in this article are from this translation.

Acknowledgment: Special thanks to Dallas Hill for participating as uke in photos and to David Runkle for photography used in the technical sections.

· 12 ·

Silat-Based Randai Theatre of West Sumatra Makes Its U.S. Debut
by Kirstin A. Pauka, Ph.D.

Photos courtesy of Kirstin Pauka. Those showing the theatre performance were taken by Tom Levy.

Introduction

Silat is the indigenous martial art found throughout Malaysia and Indonesia, with myriad regional styles of great diversity. The silat style found in West Sumatra as practiced by the Minangkabau ethnic group is also called *silek* in the Minang language, and has twelve recognized major regional styles (Pauka, 1986a & b). *Randai* theatre, the indigenous Minangkabau theatre form, is fundamentally based on silat techniques and aesthetics. Besides martial arts, Randai features dance, acting, singing, instrumental music, and a unique type of percussion played by the dancers on their pants while dancing. Randai training and performance are community-centered activities, based symbolically and also quite literally on a circle. Randai's main functions in the village community are education and entertainment. Spiritual aspects central to silat training also carry over into Randai training and performance, especially into the structure of the learning process and into the relationships between teachers and students.

This chapter focuses on the use of silat training in Randai theatre as it was experienced in the US for the first time, during an extended artist-in-residence program in the Asian Theatre Program at the University of Hawai'i.

For this six-month program, two West Sumatra master artists were resident in the Theatre and Dance Department to train students in silat and Randai: Musra Dahrizal,[2] Randai artist and silat master; and Hasanawi,[3] Minangkabau music expert. The intensive training period culminated in the first-ever English language performances of Randai in the US in February 2001.

Silat and Randai Training in the Asian Theatre Program at the University of Hawai'i

The University of Hawai'i Asian Theatre Program has a long history of hosting distinguished Asian performing artists for lengthy residencies during which theatre, dance, and music students learn a specific Asian dance-drama genre in intensive 6–12 month training programs. The training process culminates in public performances of an Asian play in English, such as Japanese Kabuki, Chinese Xingqu, Balinese Kecak, and Indian Sanskrit plays. Over the years, many of these productions have included fighting scenes based on traditional martial arts from the individual region.

In the academic year 2000–2001, the Asian theatre genre selected for this program was a "historical first": Sumatran Randai. The training and production program of this Randai faced many unique challenges. A Randai play had never been done in English in the US, had rarely been learned by non-Indonesian students, and almost never been seen by a Western audience. The guest artists were traditional folk practitioners, who had never taught in a US university system, and had never taught foreign students. In addition, Randai is strongly based in martial arts and thereby poses additional challenges in terms of high physical demands on the students and the underlying spiritual and often mystical teachings. How would Western students absorb and modify this "foreign" form?

In the last decade, cross-cultural exchanges between Asian and US theatre artists and multicultural productions and workshops have become commonplace in the US and abroad. Along with this proliferation, questions about true cross-cultural learning and cross-cultural understandings and misunderstandings are being raised. How can one tailor and guide the complex process of learning a foreign theatre or martial arts genre? How do we translate language, customs, cultural values, spiritual teachings, musical conventions, and theatrical expression so that the process is mutually beneficial for participants, teachers, and audiences, and also create performances with high production standards?

In the case of silat and Randai training, the spiritual connection that was established between the teachers and students was, in my opinion, one of the main reasons for the project's success. The thorough grounding in silat's practice and spiritual teachings offered the students a vital and direct link to the essence of Randai. For instance, cleansing ceremonies that were done for the cast members by silat master Musra Dahrizal were crucial points in the development of the group into true *anak Randai* (children of Randai). With this, the "circle" of the new Randai community became a living reality for the students. The connection between teachers and students became those of master and apprentice in the full sense of the word.

Besides the silat training and spiritual essence underlying Randai, how is silat actually incorporated into a Randai performance? All the circular *galombang* dances are based on basic silat steps and gestures, but they are clearly choreographed and executed in time to the musical accompaniment of the orchestra and singers, thereby becoming more dance-like. In addition, pure fighting sequences are frequently included in those dances, typically at the end of a sung verse. These *jurusan* sequences consist of set attack-defense moves with punches, kicks, counterpunches, kicks, locks, and escapes, most frequently executed by all dancers arranged in pairs. Most basic silat maneuvers find their way into jurusan at some point in the play. Most plays feature at least one major fighting scene, part of which is generally choreographed, and part of which is free fighting, depending on the performers' skill level. Our story actually featured a sub-plot in which the main hero, Umbuik Mudo, goes off to study with a famous silat teacher, thereby giving ample opportunity to feature actual silat training sessions and silat competitions as part of the play.

As we have seen, silat is the basis for all movement, rhythm, and aesthetic in Randai theatre; therefore, basic silat training is mandatory for all Randai performers. In the University of Hawai'i production, all cast members (actors, dancers, and even musicians) had to participate in basic silat training. Basic silat steps and attack-defense sequences (*jurusan*) were taught to the dancers and actors in preparation for the movements and fighting sequences of the dance sequences central in Randai performances, called *galombang*. Additional, more advanced training sessions were held for those actors who performed longer fighting scenes. The photos below show examples of several basic silat steps as well as more advanced combinations of defense moves from the Silek Tuo style that were part of the silat training at the University of Hawai'i.[4]

Documentation of Silat Techniques

SECTION 1
Examples of single-handed defenses against single strikes

Basic single-handed attacks can be countered either via the inside or outside of the attacking arm, with a same-side block or a cross block. All blocks usually have multiple follow-up options. The photos below show a few of those possibilities.

Photo 1: The attacker on the left (student) attacks with a straight punch to the solar plexus. The defender (Musra Dahrizal) uses a single-handed block to the inside of the attacker's wrist, while simultaneously stepping off the line of attack to the inside.

Photo 2: Same attack. The defender uses a single-handed cross-block to the inside of the attacker's wrist and grabs the wrist for a follow-up technique.

Photos 3a, b, c: Same attack. The defender uses a single-handed block to the outside of the attacker's wrist, and grabs it in preparation for follow-up techniques. A quick shuffle step closes the gap to the attacker, the initial wrist grab remains in place while the defender readies his other arm for an elbow strike to the opponent's elbow (3b), or chin (3c).

SECTION 2

Examples of double-handed defenses against single strikes

Photo 4a, b, c: Following a single-handed attack, the defender grabs and twists the wrist with both hands. Applying pressure to the joint through twisting and pressing inward (4b), he forces his opponent to the ground. An optional follow-up to this take-down is a shuffle step to close the gap and a combination of neck twist and knee strike to the opponent's elbow.

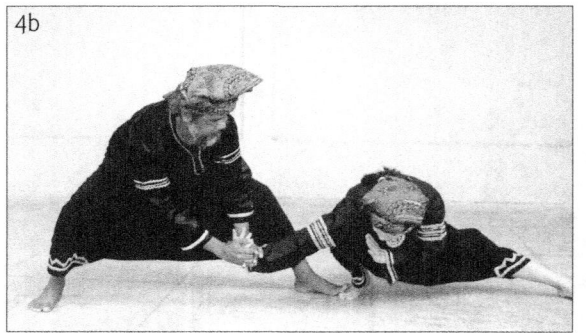

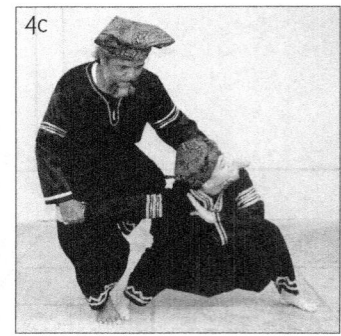

Photos 5a, b: Following a single-handed grab attack, the defender (the student) rotates her hand forward and out to twist the attacker's arm, then moves in to apply pressure to the outside of the attackers elbow which leads to a take-down. Notice the teacher's set-up for another counterattack by lodging his foot behind the heel of the student from where he could execute a leg sweep and reverse the wrist lock on her. Ideally, advanced practitioners can continue to "play" (*main terus*) countering each counterattack again and again, which can go on for a time, using variations of the basic wrist, elbow, and shoulder locks to unbalance their training partner.

Photo 6

Instead of moving to the elbow for the take-down as demonstrated in Photo 5b, the teacher shows another option here: by applying pressure to the back of the student's shoulder joint, he can unbalance her and achieve a similar but lower take-down.

SECTION 3
Examples of defenses against kicks

Photo 7: The attacker on the right (student) attacks with a straight kick. The defender catches the foot and applies pressure to the toes, unbalancing the opponent.

Photo 8: Same attack. The defender steps off the line of attack toward the inside, catches the foot with both hands, and applies pressure to the inside of the foot, forcing the opponent to rotate and lose balance.

Photo 9: A variation to the technique shown in Photo 8. Here, the second hand applies pressure to the knee instead of to the side of the foot, in preparation for a take-down.

Photo 10: Same attack. The defender steps off the line to the outside, catches the foot with both hands, and applies pressure to the outside of the foot, with a similar effect as in Photo 8.

Photo 11a, b: A variation of the defense from the outside. Here the second hand applies pressure to the knee instead of the side of the foot, with the same result as in Photo 9. Shown here is the follow-up take-down that results from the continued pressure applied to the side of the knee.

SECTION 4
Examples of kick defenses against single-handed strikes

Photo 12: Attacker (right) strikes with a straight punch to the solar plexus. The defender quickly moves off to the outside and checks the attacker's arm at the elbow. A possible follow-up here is to kick the elbow, resulting in the attacker losing balance.

Photo 13: The same technique as in Photo 12, except that the defensive kick is applied to the inside of the attacker's elbow.

SECTION 5
Examples of double defenses against double attacks (hand and foot)

Photo 14: Double outside cross-block with hand and foot, crossing at the wrist and ankle respectively. This technique is often used in basic exercises during which the students move backwards and forwards across the floor, retaining the proper fighting distance. As a defense, it sets up any number of follow-up techniques, similar to single-handed attacks.

Photo 15: The attacker punches and kicks simultaneously, the defender (right) blocks the kick to the outside with the hand (hidden from view behind the teacher's thigh) and uses a one-handed defense against the punch, similar to single-hand defenses, here with an inside variation of the wrist grab.

Photo 16: The attacker kicks and simultaneously executes a knifehand strike to the temple. The defender enters inside with a body turn that allows him to catch the leg, while at the same time extending the other hand for a counter-strike to the throat. This is a difficult technique only taught to students at the intermediate level.

Photo 17: Same attack. The defender moves to the outside with a body twist, and catches the leg and arm together to immobilize the attacker. Like the technique in Photo 16, this is also an advanced technique. Both are executed rapidly and depend on accurate timing so that the opponent's leg can be caught before the kick is retracted.

SECTION 6
Examples of advanced head-hold techniques

Photo 18: An advanced head-twisting technique is applied as a counterattack to the high foot-locking technique shown in photo 17. Both hands twist the head to one side, forcing the opponent to release the hold on the leg.

Photo 19: A similar head-twisting technique is used against a similar hold on the foot, here at a lower level than in photo 18.

Photo 20: A head-locking technique is applied as a defense against a kick. The head-lock here is the follow-up technique to a quick evasive move in which the defender jumps to the other side of the attacker, thereby evading the kick, and unbalancing the opponent.

Photo 21: Another example of an evasive move to a punch brings the defender (left) behind the attacker from where he can execute a controlling head-lock.

SECTION 6
Silat in Randai performance

The following photos show examples of silat elements in Randai performance.

Photo 22: The opening formation of a Randai performance is often done in lines that later spread out into a circle. Here, the performers enter in three lines. Once in place, the dancers perform a fast-paced silat sequence. The dancers from both outside lines alternatingly attack the dancers in the center line. This creates an exciting opening number and sets a lively mood for what follows.

Photo 23: The basic circle formation of a Randai performance. The dancers move counter-clockwise around the circle using silat steps, turns, and hand gestures, accompanied by a song and flute piece.

Photo 24: Circle formations can be doubled, with an inner and outer circle for variety. The dancers here perform the signature technique of Randai, the percussive pants-slapping while dancing (*tapuak*).

Photo 25: A close-up of silat steps as done during the *galombang* dance in preparation of an attack-defense sequence with a partner.

Photo 26—29: These photos show various silat elements of the jurusan sequences, attack-defense sections done by all dancers simultaneously and in time to the circle leader's vocal cues.

Photo 26: A straight punch is countered by a grab and elbow strike.

Photo 27: A double kick is executed by both dancers simultaneously, and countered by one of them with an open-handed block (hidden from view behind the left dancer's thigh).

Photo 28 and 29: A straight kick is countered by a grab and knee twist. This leads to the take-down (in 28) of the dancer on the right. She then counters with a backwards kick, a recovering step backwards, followed by a double elbow strike.

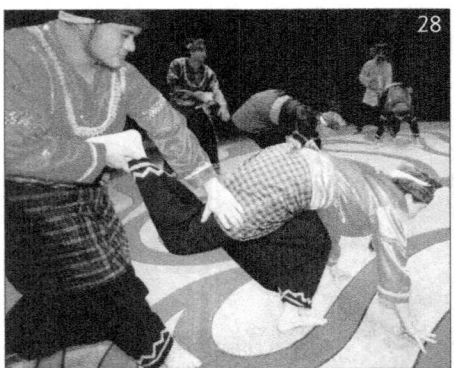

Photos 30 and 31: Fighting sequences are part of the acting in Randai and constitute a prominent feature of Randai theatre. In photo 30, the silat master teacher demonstrates a sequence during dress rehearsal. Photo 31: Both actors engage in a choreographed fighting scene during a performance.

Notes

1. Musra Dahrizal, a native of Padang Panjang, West Sumatra, is a well-known traditional Minangkabau artist and an expert in silat, flute (*saluang*) music, and Randai theatre. Since 1991, he has been leading the Randai group "Palito Nyalo," one of the foremost Randai groups in West Sumatra today. Currently, he is also leading the "Rambun Sati" group. Besides actively practicing and teaching silat and Randai, Dahrizal is also a highly sought after saluang and dendang singing performer; he has recorded seven audio cassettes of saluang music.
2. Like many Indonesians, Hasanawi goes by only one name. A native of Batusangkar, West Sumatra, he is a master teacher of traditional Minangkabau music, especially saluang, and other wind instruments like *bansi* and *sarunai*, as well as *gendang* drums and the traditional Minangkabau bronze percussion (*talempong*). This music is also used to accompany silat practice and performance. Silat students are expected to learn this music as well.
3. These examples are by no means intended as a complete overview of Silek Tuo techniques of the Minangkabau, which is far beyond the scope of this chapter.

Additional Reading

Pauka, K. (1986a). Silek: The martial arts of the Minangkabau in West Sumatra. *Journal of Asian Martial Arts*, 6(1), 62–79.

Pauka, K. (1986b). A flower of martial arts: The Randai folk theatre of the Minangkabau in West Sumatra. *Journal of Asian Martial Arts*, 6(4), 10–29.

index

aikijutsu, 139-140
aikido, 88-90, 92-93
Akaoka Daisuke, 8
Anazawa-ryu, 8, 29
Araki-ryu, 31
Art of War, 138-139
atarashi naginata, 17, 24-25, 27-30, 32
baguazhang, 104
bo (long-staff), 29, 130
Boenisch, Yvonne, 98-100
Book of Change (*Yijing*), 88-91, 93
Boshin Senso civil war, 7-8
Brazilian jiujitsu, 32
Chang Xiangyu, 39
Cheng Yanqiu, 42
Chholia dance, 61
Dai Nippon Butokukai, 10, 14
Daito-ryu, 8
Dandiya Raas (stick dance) 62-63
Epitaph for Wang Zhengnan, 104
eskrima, 79
femininity, 4, 17, 109-110
Fuxing Peking Opera School, 39-40, 42
Gai Jiaotian, 39
Gair, 62
Ge Hong, 106 note 2
Geendad, 62
gekiken kogyo, 14, 19-20
Gempei War, 113
Ghumura, 65-66, 71
Hangaku Gozen, 2-3
Hasanawi, 155, 167 note 2
Heckler, Richard, 93
Heike Monogatari, 2
Higashi Tomoko, 16
Himeji Normal College, 21
Hojo katas, 13
Huang Zongxi, 104
iaido, 14
Ichi Monji no Midare, 10-11
internal/external martial arts, 88, 104-105

Itto-ryu, 8, 19,
Jikishinkage-ryu, 13-17, 19, 24-25, 29
jo (mid-length staff), 10
Ka Shad Mastieh (sword dance), 67
kabuki theater, 107-118, 155
kalarippayaatu, 63
kamayari (long-hafted sickle), 9
karate, 21, 139
Karyu Sodezaki, 109
Kashima Shinto-ryu, 9, 13
Katori Shinto-ryu, 19
kathakali, 57, 71, 133-134
kendo, 14, 16-18, 21, 24
kenjutsu, 8-9
kiai (use of breath/voice), 12-13, 16
Kim Il Sung, 101
Kobayashi Seiko, 20, 23
Komatsuzaki Koto, 19
Kurokochi Dengoro, 8
kusarigama, 10, 16, 20
Kyu Sun Hui, 97-101
Leonard, George, 92, 94
Li Shaochun, 46
Li Xiaoping, 38
Long Boxing (*changquan*), 46
Love's Snowbound Barrier Gate, 111
Lupetey, Yurisle, 100
Madama Butterfly, 108-109
Maiden of Yue, 102-106
Manikeswari, 65
marriage and martial art theory, 88-96
martial art theory, 14, 102-105
Matsudaira Katamori, 8
Matsudaira Teruhime, 8
Matsumoto Bizen no Kami, 113
Mehr Rass, 62-63
Mei Lanfang, 42
Minamoto no Yoritomo, 113
Minamoto no Yoshitsune, 113
Mirror Mountain: A Women's Treasury of Loyalty, 116-118

Mitamura Chiyo, 10-11, 29
Mitamura Kengyo, 10-11, 13, 29
Mitamura Takeko, 11
Murakami Hideo, 19-20
Muromachi era, 2, 32
Muay Thai, 32
Muhen-ryu, 29-30
Musra Dahrizal, 155-157, 167
naginata, 1-36, 111, 114-115, 117
nagamaki, 31
Nakano Takeko, 7-8
National Theater of Japan, 108, 117
Nitta Suzuyo, 23, 31, 33
onnagata (female role players), 108-112, 116-118
Paika dance, 66
Pathet-Haiba, 68-69
Peking Opera, 37-43, 45-49, 53
pendulum motion, 80-82
percussive pants-slapping (*tapuak*), 165
Pharikhand Khela, 70
puppet play (*bunraku*), 107, 113
push hands, 93
Randai theatre, 154
random flow training, 79-81
Rookmar, 70
Ryugo-ryu, 14
Saito Denkibo Katsuhide, 9-11, 13
Sakakida Yaeko, 21, 24
Satake Shigeo, 14, 16
Satake Yoshinori, 14
Seitokusha school, 10
Sengoku Jidai (Warring States Period 1467-1573), 4
Shimada Teruko, 14-15
shinai (split bamboo replica sword), 14, 16, 18, 21, 25, 27
Shinkage-ryu, 13, 19
Shizuga-ryu, 19
Shinto-ryu, 13
Shubukan Dojo, 11, 13
Showa period (1926-1989), 21
silat, 154-167
silek, 154, 156
Silek Tuo style, 156 note 3

Sonobe Hideo, 14, 16, 21
Sonobe Masami, 15
Sonobe Shigehachi, 14
spear, 3, 10, 19, 34 note, 60, 67-69, 109-110, 115, 117
Spring and Autumn Annals, 102
stage fighting, 37, 39, 41, 45-46, 53-54, 60-61, 69, 108-112, 114-117, 124
Sudhakaran, T., 121-122, 124, 126-132, 134-135
Sunzi, 138-140, 144, 146, 148-150, 152-153
Takeda Sokaku, 8
Tang Wenhua, 42
taijiquan, 39, 88-89, 92-96, 104
Takenouchi-ryu, 34 note 3
Ten-ryu, 9, 11, 13
Tendo-ryu, 9-13, 21, 24-26, 28-29, 34 note 10, 114
Thang Ta, 68-69
Thich Nhat Hanh, 92, 94-95
Toda-ha Buko-ryu, 5, 19-23, 31
Tohei, Koichi, 89
Tomoe Gozen, 1-2, 34 note 1
Toya Akiko, 15-16
Three-Forked Crossroad, 37, 49, 53-54
Treasury of Loyal Retainers, 107, 116-117
Tsukahara Bokuden, 9
Umpad, Sonny, 79
universal post posture, 94-95
Vaar Geet, 60
Visayan Corto Kadena Eskrima, 79
University of Hawai'i, 154-156
Werbrouck, Ulla, 73-78
wugong (martial-acrobatic arts), 38, 40, 47, 51
xingyiquan, 104
Yamada Heizaemon Mitsunori, 13
Yamamoto Yaeko, 8, 34 note 9
Yazawa Isao, 5, 19, 21
Yoshitsune and the Thousand Cherry Trees, 113
Zhu Luhao, 37-38, 42

Printed in Great Britain
by Amazon